URBAN VIEWS

12 Quilts Inspired by City Living

CHERRI HOUSE

stashBOOKS.
an imprint of C&T Publishing

Text copyright © 2013 by Cherri House

Photography and Artwork copyright © 2013 by C&T Publishing, Inc.

Publisher | Amy Marson

Creative Director | Gailen Runge

Art Director / Cover Designer | Kristy Zacharias

Editors | Cynthia Bix and Phyllis Elving

Technical Editors | Susan Nelsen and Nanette Zeller

Book Designer | April Mostek

Page Layout Artist | Kerry Graham

Production Coordinator | Jenny Davis

Production Editor | Joanna Burgarino

Illustrator | Jenny Davis

Photography by Christina Carty-Francis and Diane Pedersen of C&T Publishing, Inc., unless otherwise noted

Published by Stash Books, an imprint of C&T Publishing, Inc., P.O. Box 1456, Lafayette, CA 94549

Library of Congress Cataloging-in-Publication Data

House, Cherri.

Urban views : 12 quilts inspired by city living / by Cherri House.

pages cm

ISBN 978-1-60705-541-9 (soft cover)

1. Patchwork--Patterns. 2. Quilting--Patterns. 3. City and town life in art. I. Title.

TT835.H667 2013

746.46--dc23

2012040226

Printed in China

10 9 8 7 6 5 4 3 2 1

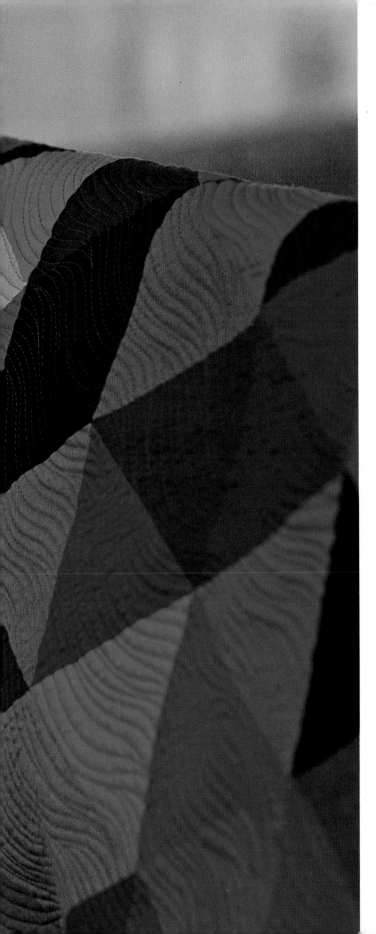

DEDICATION

To Lizzy—thank you
for being the teacher.

To Rich—my dearest friend,
you are the best!

ACKNOWLEDGMENTS

To Cynthia Bix—I'm so happy
to work with you again!

To C&T Publishing—thank you so much
for the privilege of creating this book.

Thank you, Robert Kaufman—your
fabrics bring my quilting dreams to life.

Thank you to Ann, Brooke, and Melissa—
my sewing/ironing team

Thank you, Angela Walters, the
wunderkind of the quilting world!

Thank you, Phyllis Elving and
Susan Nelsen—your patience and
guidance are greatly appreciated.

CONTENTS

Foreword by Kathy Mack . . . 6

Preface 7

NEW CITY QUILTS 8

More Grids! 10

Expanding on the Theme . . 14
Playing with Blocks, 17

Triangles
—Adding to the Mix 17

Fabrics: Solids
and Near-Solids 19
Creating Strips with Solids, 22

Working with Color 23
Color-Wise, 24

Elements of Design 25
*Simplicity in Art by David Jones
and Lisa Jones, 26*

Quilting Makes the Quilt . . 28

The City Challenge 30

THE QUILTS 32

City Rain 35

City Trail 41

City Bridge 47

City Woods 53

City Hall 59

City Traffic 63

City Sky 67

City Loft 71

City Recycling . . 75

City Beat 81

City Electric 87

City Lake 93

QUILTMAKING ESSENTIALS 99

Useful Techniques 100
Pressing • Rotary cutting • Construction • Pinning

Finishing Basics 104
Borders • Backing • Batting • Layering • Basting • Quilting • Binding

Quilt Color List 108

Resources 110

About the Author 110
Teaching: A Two-Way Street, 111

FOREWORD

Five years ago, I opened my fabric store with 30 much-beloved colors of Kona Cotton. The grand scheme was to expand that well-curated selection as interest in quiltmaking with solids grew. Of course, I had ulterior motives. I love using solids in my quilts and dreamed of having an endless selection of color in my own backyard!

The next influx of new colors came in the form of 20 bolts based on the supply list of Cherri House's *City Park* quilt pattern, one of my all-time best-selling patterns and a personal favorite. When the boxes arrived I stacked the fabrics all together on the table. What a display of color! It left no doubt in my mind that Cherri was blazing a trail in contemporary quilt design using only solid fabrics. I appreciated that each of her patterns showcased a diverse color palette, clever block construction, and expert placement of value with solids. This gal was onto something!

I eagerly awaited the release of Cherri's first book, *City Quilts*. Reading it cover to cover left me amazed, inspired, and full of ideas about making quilts with solid fabrics. I also discovered a like-minded soul, someone who would soon become my friend, who makes quilts from her heart. All of Cherri's designs would look spectacular hanging on the wall, but that is not the intent. They are made to be used, loved, and given freely.

Urban Views picks up where *City Quilts* left off. It takes us farther into color theory and teaches more advanced design techniques. The popularity of quilting with solids continues to grow. *Urban Views* is a timely and much-needed book for the new wave of quilters exploring what modern quilting means to them. Each project offers a lesson in designing with solids. Cherri's uncanny ability to bring unexpected colors into harmony surprises, delights, and results in spectacular quilts you'll want to make and wrap around someone you love.

The solids wall at Pink Chalk Fabrics now boasts more than 400 colors from a wide variety of manufacturers. Yes, the interest in quilting with solids is stronger than ever, and it's coupled with creative enthusiasm for exploring the possibilities of designing in the absence of prints. With this book, my talented friend Cherri House welcomes us into her unique world of making exciting solid quilts and teaches us by example what those possibilities can be … a valuable gift we can each take along on our own quilt-making journey.

—Kathy Mack

Quilter and pattern designer Kathy Mack operates the online shop Pink Chalk Fabrics.

PREFACE

The journey that began with *City Quilts* continues! Thank you so much for your warm reception of *City Quilts*, published in 2010. Your stories of creating city quilts, whether for yourself or for your loved ones, bring a smile to my face. Many of you have begun using and loving solids for the first time, which is awesome. Maybe best of all are the emails and comments telling me about how you are seeing your neighborhoods and cities as never before. You've taken the everyday and ordinary, and turned them into original works of art!

City Quilts was about my journey as a quilter, and the city where I live—the inspiration that led to twelve abstract interpretations of everyday scenes in Houston, Texas. *Urban Views* picks up where *City Quilts* left off, exploring new fabric choices, new blocks, new skills, and even some new cities.

Urban Views is also a reflection of the comments and questions I've received from you through my teaching and speaking opportunities over the last year. Many thanks to all of you who have shared your sincere thoughts and feelings about your love of quilting, fabric, color, and life. My life is richer for having met you!

Cherri House

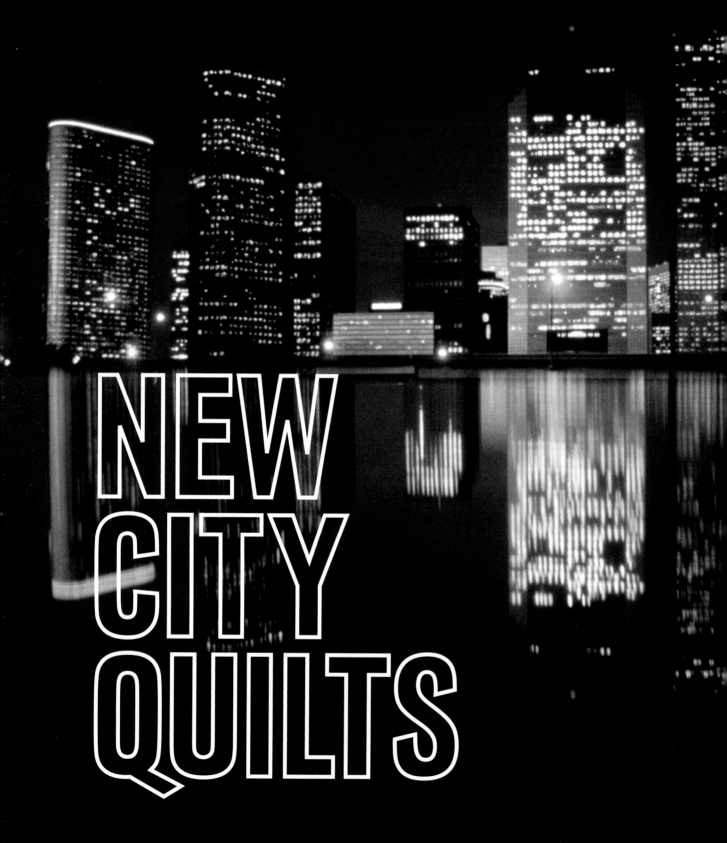

NEW CITY QUILTS

When *City Quilts* was completed, I thought it was finished. I thought, "I've created all the city quilts I'm going to make; I'll move on to something new." Not so. The new quilts I was designing weren't "me," and the only things I wanted to make were more city quilts. Several months and about 50 less-than-wonderful designs later, I gave up the fight of trying to create something more complex, with intricate pieced blocks, and started putting on paper the quilts that I loved. Why did I believe that something more complex would be better? Why had I been putting limitations on my creativity, which is exactly what I preach against? So much internal drama.

Once I gave myself permission to create what I really wanted, the floodgates opened! Along with the flood of ideas also came the challenge of how to create a book that built on the foundation of *City Quilts* but wasn't just more of the same. Among the ways I chose to move forward were to add a variety of triangles to the mix and to look at the fabric options offered by near-solids, hand-dyes, and cross-weaves. Another important addition to this book is you! You've helped to shape this book, and I thank you!

MORE GRIDS!

The quilts in this book, like those in *City Quilts*, are created using a grid system. Whether they are simple or complex, grids provide the structure and foundation for a balanced design composition. Utilizing a gridded format works for modern and traditional quilters alike.

The beauty of working with grids is the limitless possibilities offered within each new framework. The most basic of grids consists of squares. While a square is a simple shape, what occurs within the blocks—in terms of colors, secondary patterns, and overall design—obscures the minimal nature of the grid.

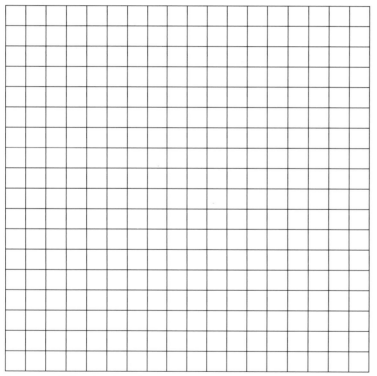

Square grid for *City Recycling*

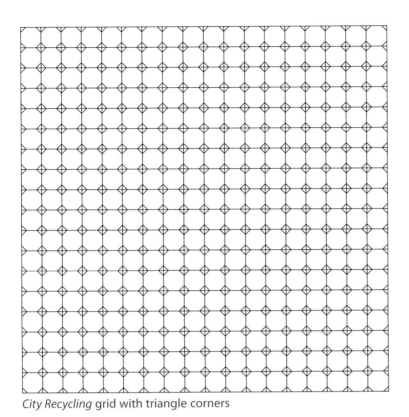

City Recycling grid with triangle corners

City Recycling (page 75) begins as a simple square grid. Corner triangles add a secondary element, the consistent use of off-white as background color unifies the entire piece, and the gridded use of color creates diagonal lines that contribute another design element. Broken down to the basic elements, *City Recycling* is made up of Snowball blocks (Cutting Corners, page 77) sewn together in a nine-patch configuration.

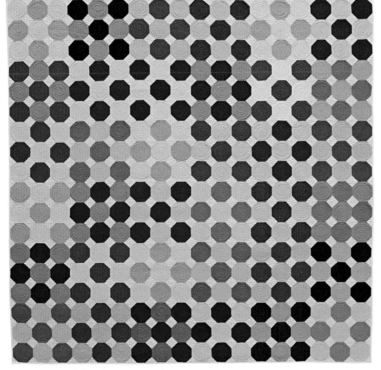

City Recycling (full quilt on page 75)

City Traffic (page 63) is built on a basic grid of rectangles. With this quilt, the first thing the eye sees is the grid itself. The use of black as a background color draws your focus to the body of the quilt. The black sashing separating the blocks and rows is negative space, while the bursts of color in the blocks create movement.

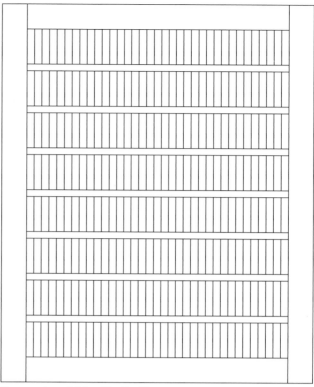

Rectangle grid for *City Traffic*

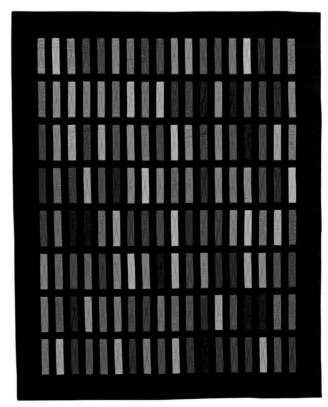

City Traffic (full quilt on page 63)

Rectangle grid for *City Sky*

Another grid of rectangles is used for *City Sky* (page 67), for a completely different effect. With no sashing or spacing between the blocks, colors flow from block to block. Through the manipulation of color, some blocks appear to be taller or shorter than others, but they are actually all the same size. The illusion of varying heights causes the viewer to pause and take a closer look at this quilt.

City Sky (full quilt on page 67)

EXPANDING ON THE THEME

Traditional pieced or appliquéd blocks, used in a gridded format, are the basis of traditional quilts. But new creative opportunities appear when you utilize a traditional block—or your own original block—in a grid with the intention of expanding beyond the boundaries of the shape. A Flying Geese block becomes a bridge, Snowball blocks become a stack of glass bottles, and a simple circle appliquéd in a square becomes a forest.

City Bridge (full quilt on page 47)

A photorealistic quilt would replicate an object in very fine detail, whether it be a face, a landscape, or an animal. The goal would be to produce a fabricated piece that looked just like the subject matter. In contrast, these urban quilts are born by creating a design based on the *essence* of an object—the abstraction of the idea. Instead of literal translations of images, the quilts pull from feelings, senses, mood, light, and energy. The goal is to have the quilt speak to the viewer and to have the viewer recognize a connection to the object that inspired the quilt designer. All of the quilt's components—fabric, design, block construction, quilting—contribute to the overall composition.

To construct a quilt inspired by an object using a gridded foundation, you must first find—or design—a block that works for the piece. While driving on a bridge in Portland, I immediately thought, "That looks like a Flying Geese block." Years later when I decided to create a quilt honoring Portland, I knew exactly what the block needed to be. It was the perfect fit!

TIP *A good reference book on traditional quilt blocks can be very helpful for finding blocks to fit the roles you want them to play in a city quilt.*

City Woods (full quilt on page 53)

In creating a quilt to represent Boston, my inspiration was the city's Freedom Trail, with its red stone markers. I searched for a block that would translate this idea; finding none, I created my own simple block that looks like a path. The red fabric throughout *City Trail* (page 41) represents the stones along the trail.

City Trail (full quilt on page 41)

Jemma was a quilt I created to showcase the fabrics of Lonni Rossi. These fabrics looked like little jewels to me, so I needed a block that looked like faceted jewels. In the end I used the tried-and-true Bow Tie block, half of it with the jeweled fabric and the other half with a near-solid. A little deconstructing of blocks is a clever way to find a block to fill a need.

Jemma, 63˝ × 63˝, machine pieced by Cherri House

Playing with Blocks

A fun creative exercise is to take a traditional block and see how many variations you can come up with by changing out fabric, turning the block on the diagonal, and making it over-sized or very small. Experiment with the use of sashing, or try alternating a pieced block with a plain block to see what patterns appear. This kind of play can be done with pen and graph paper or computer quilting software (I use EQ7—see Resources, page 110), or by sewing some blocks and playing around with them on a design wall.

Something to keep in mind when designing blocks is how they will be pieced and joined together for the quilt top. Look for ways to minimize pressing and seam issues.

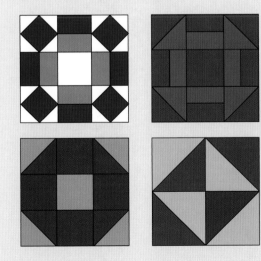

TRIANGLES— ADDING TO THE MIX

The addition of triangles is a natural progression in a quilting skill set. Creating trian-gles requires advanced rotary cutting skills as well as precise sewing and careful pressing techniques. Mastering the skills to create triangles opens a whole new world of options for your sewn creations.

Triangles commonly used in quilting include half-square triangles, 60° triangles, and isosceles triangles. Half-square triangles are sewn from fabric squares, while 60° and isos-celes triangles are created from fabric strips using specialty rulers or templates.

Half-Square Triangles

Half-square triangles are made by pairing two fabric squares, right sides together, as follows. This technique is used to make the Flying Geese units for *City Bridge* (page 47) and also the Snowball patches for *City Recycling* (page 75).

City Lake, made with 60° triangles (full quilt on page 93)

1. Lightly draw a line diagonally from one corner to the opposite corner on the wrong side of one square.

Draw line.

2. Sew a scant ¼˝ seam on each side of the line.

Sew.

3. Cut on the drawn line.

4. Press open carefully to avoid stretching the bias edge. Trim off the dog-ears.

60° Triangles

A 60° triangle is also called an equilateral triangle. The sides are all equal lengths, and each angle equals 60°. These units are easy to cut from strips of fabric using a 60° specialty ruler or a template, as shown in the directions for *City Lake* (page 93).

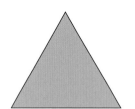

Equilateral (60°) triangle: equal angles and sides

Isosceles Triangles

An isosceles triangle has two equal-length sides and two angles that are the same. Like 60° triangles, these are cut from fabric strips with the aid of a specialty ruler or a template—see *City Electric* (page 87).

Isosceles triangle: two equal angles and two equal sides

FABRICS: SOLIDS AND NEAR-SOLIDS

Just as the grid has been expanded for *Urban Views*, I'm suggesting some new fabric possibilities to consider along with my perennial-favorite solids. All of the city quilts can be successfully interpreted with near-solid prints, cross-weaves, batiks, and hand-dyed fabrics as well as solids.

While solids and near-solids can appear similar on the surface, structurally there are differences unique to the various fabrics within this grouping.

Solid-color fabrics

Cross-weave fabrics

Solid and cross-weave fabrics have solid-color warp and weft threads or yarn running throughout, so the fabric looks the same on the front and the back. *Solid fabrics* such as Robert Kaufman's Kona Cotton Solids, with their uniform color and texture, are excellent for use in modern or Amish-style quilts, or combined with print fabrics. *Two-color woven fabrics* use two different-colored threads for the warp and the weft, creating subtle variations in color. Examples include chambray, Moda Cross Weaves, Westminster Shot Cottons, and some dupioni silks.

Near-solid fabrics (such as Robert Kaufman Quilter's Linen or Free Spirit Designer Essentials) appear solid from a distance but are actually printed on one side, like any other print fabric. Up close, the variations in color and texture are evident. These tone-on-tone fabrics are printed in a variety of patterns—stripes, dots, florals, and so on. Manufacturers create entire lines of near-solids as well as adding them to other fabric collections.

Hand-dyed and batik fabrics begin as solid-colored fabrics but are then immersed in dye to give them additional coloration. Hand-dyes have a deep saturation of color as a result of the dyeing process. The appearance of hand-dyed fabrics ranges from solid to multicolored. Near-solid hand-dyes have a very organic texture and work as beautiful alternatives to solid fabrics. Hand-painted fabrics can also range from solid to multicolored.

Hand-dyed and hand-painted fabrics

Any and all of these fabrics can be used to create any of the city quilts, depending on the effect you want to achieve. The photos below show examples of the same quilt design carried out with different types of fabric: *The Tempest* was made using Kona Cotton Solids, and *Silk Tempest* was made from similar-colored silks.

The Tempest, 71″ × 89″, machine pieced by Cherri House and machine quilted by DeLoa Jones

Silk Tempest, 59″ × 59″, machine pieced and quilted by Cherri House

Each fabric has its own unique set of properties. Create practice blocks from various types of fabrics to ensure that you'll end up with the results you are seeking.

When Near-Solids Are Best

Yes, I actually said it—it's true. Sometimes near-solids work better than my beloved solids! One of my favorite quilts is *House's House*, made with Moda Grunge by Basic Grey. I love this fabric, and when I saw it I knew exactly what I wanted to make: a house quilt. This fabric was the perfect choice for the house and neighborhood that I envisioned, a little on the "I've seen better days" side of things. The grunge fabric created a neighborhood that felt well lived in, and worn. This quilt could be made with solids to create an entirely different effect, depending on the colors chosen. When considering your fabric selection, keep in mind the entire composition and mood that you are trying to create.

House's House, 59˝ × 65˝, machine pieced and quilted by Cherri House

Creating Strips with Solids

Creating long fabric strips from prints—for sashing or bindings, for instance—is a basic sewing skill. Creating continuous strips from solids, batiks, or hand-dyes is a little more challenging. The challenge lies in the fact that there's no right or wrong side of the fabric.

Begin by deciding on what you want to be the "right" side for your project. Mark it with a sticker, a piece of masking tape, a safety pin—anything that works to identify the right side for you.

1. Lay the first strip, "right" side up, on a rotary cutting mat. Lay the end of a second strip over the end of the first strip, "wrong" side up, at a 90° angle to the first strip.

Right sides together

2. Mark a diagonal line for stitching, as shown. Pin to secure the strips.

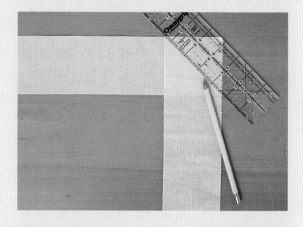

3. Fold back the top strip at the marked stitching line. This now becomes the right side of the strip.

4. Continue the process of adding to the strip until it is as long as you need for the project.

5. Stitch all the pinned segments together. Join the pieced strip to the quilt as normal, according to the project directions. Press and trim the seams.

WORKING WITH COLOR

Fabrics function much like paint. You can add sparkle, light, and interest through the colors you choose. If you come from a traditional quilting background, your typical fabric selection process may begin with choosing a focus fabric. But a different mind-set may be needed when working with solids and near-solids. Instead of a focus fabric, you may have a focus color or theme.

Can you ever have too many colors in one quilt? Probably, but I'll stretch the limit every time. I love color … the more the better. Be brave and push the color envelope where possible. If the main color is red, extend along the color wheel to orange on one side and purple on the other, and use everything in between. Your compositions will have much more depth and variety as a result.

Background fabrics are usually considered neutral elements, but they are really the foundation for the entire piece. They determine how all of the colors play together, and they give the quilt its tone. In *City Rain* (page 35), the dark gray background sets off all the other colors, making them sparkle. The light background of *City Recycling* (page 75) serves to unify the many different colors in the piece.

TIP *Need some color inspiration? Take a walk and really look at the colors around you—if it works in nature, it will work in a quilt! Or look to the great artists. You can't go wrong using the colors in your favorite works of art. Even advertisements and product packaging can be sources of ideas. After all, companies spend big bucks getting the colors right for their marketing tools.*

Color-Wise

The color wheel—an essential tool for quilters—is a visual representation of color relationships. The three primary colors (red, yellow, and blue) are equidistant from each other on the color wheel. Between them are the three secondary colors (orange, green, and violet) and the six intermediary colors (yellow-orange, red-orange, red-violet, blue-violet, blue-green, and yellow-green), all of which are created by combining the primary colors. Black, white, and gray aren't included in the color wheel.

A *complementary* color scheme pairs colors that are directly across from each other on the color wheel. An *analogous* color scheme utilizes any three colors that are side by side on the wheel. A *triadic* color scheme is three colors equally spaced around the color wheel—such as blue-green, yellow-orange, and red-violet. A *monochromatic* color scheme features a single color family in various tints, tones, and shades. (A *tint* is a color with white added, a *shade* is a color with black added, and a *tone* is a color with gray added.) A *cool* color scheme takes its colors from the "cool" half of the color wheel—blues, greens, and violets. A *warm* color scheme uses the "warm" side—reds, oranges, and yellows.

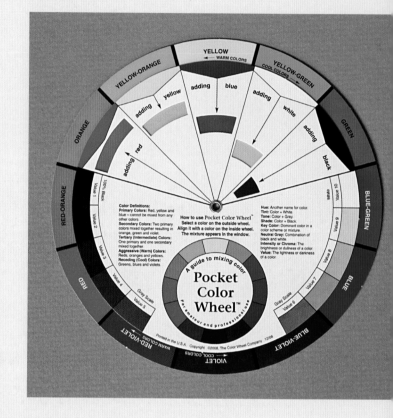

Looking for Value

To create quilts that glow with light, depth, and movement, you must have enough value and contrast in your fabrics to build intensity. Value simply means how light or dark a color is. No matter what color scheme you're using, it's essential that you include a variety of lights, mediums, and darks to create visual interest. The colors need to crescendo and decrescendo in incremental steps from the starting color—within a single block or across the entire quilt.

Color value may not be obvious until you view a fabric up against other fabrics. The Ultimate 3-in-1 Color Tool, available from C&T Publishing (see Resources, page 110), has small green and red value finders that can help determine the value contrast between fabrics.

TIP *I often choose a print backing fabric as a playful contrast to a quilt top composed of solids. The backing can be a reflection of the quilt top in terms of color or shapes—a nice bonus to the quilt you've created.*

ELEMENTS OF DESIGN

Designing a quilt means creating a piece that is both functional and aesthetically pleasing.

The most important factors in design are form (or aesthetics) and function. The *function* portion of the design process is about how the quilt will be used. This affects all the aspects of construction: the cutting, the sewing, the quilting—all of the elements that make the quilt a quilt. The *aesthetic* component of a quilt—how it looks—is very personal, and what appeals to one person may not appeal to another. A quilt that attracts an engineer may not be the same quilt that speaks to a doll collector. With an endless number of options, there's no right or wrong. It's a matter of taste and opinion.

One important element in design is a focal point—a central element designed to bring attention and emphasis to a composition. But a single focal point isn't necessary to create a successful design. Light and color can provide contrast and movement as well as visual emphasis within a piece. The city quilts in this book are purely abstract, with shape, line, and color defining the essence of the urban view that's being represented.

Simplicity in Art

I find simplicity in art beautiful; my heart sings when I see the work of Josef Albers or Mark Rothko. When I share my quilts with others, words repeatedly mentioned are *simple* and *plain*. While simple and plain aren't bad, the connotation seems to be that simple and plain work lacks substance, due to its minimalist nature. In trying to understand this mind-set, I turned to David and Lisa Jones, professional fine artists and teachers. I've asked them to share their opinion on simplicity in art from a fine arts point of view:

"We're big fans of Cherri's quilts and her great use of geometric shapes to create modern fabric compositions. Her work reminds us of the minimalist art movement of the late 60s and early 70s, an offshoot of and reaction to the highly expressive art of abstract expressionism (think Jackson Pollock). Minimalist artists such as Agnes Martin and Sol LeWitt sought to reduce their paintings to only those elements (line, shape, color) essential to the composition. The resulting works were often calm, restful, and contemplative.

When our art students are first introduced to minimalism, some are hesitant to accept it as art. A typical reaction might be to dismiss it as being simple and therefore easy to create. A work of art that has a sparse visual composition or minimal detail and decoration might elicit the modern art cliché, "That's easy; anyone could do that," suggesting that no skill is required in creating such a work.

However, when students are assigned to make their own art in this style, they begin to appreciate the skill and restraint it takes to create a successful piece. They learn that simplicity and minimalism can actually be quite complex. Reducing the number of elements you have to work with doesn't make it any easier to produce a great piece of art. If anything, the opposite is true. The less you have to work with, the harder it is to make something interesting to look at.

When you remove the visual noise created by multiple layers of pattern, texture, and color, there is less to distract the eye from the basic and real heart of the composition. Each choice the artist makes becomes even more important. Each element has to support the composition or be discarded. Deciding what to include and what to leave out, setting boundaries and limits, and especially knowing when you've reached the right balance—these are key to the success of any piece of art, and no less essential when the desired outcome is simplicity.

Cherri has mastered the art of choosing well, and she's so good at what she does that she makes it look easy to create something so perfectly simple and sophisticated. Given the endless possibilities available to quilters today, Cherri's quilts stand out as calm and restful, both modern and timeless, and that's exactly why we love her style. Our lives are busy and often far from simple, so it's refreshing and inspiring to have Cherri's designs in our home as visual reminders to slow down and embrace simplicity—in the form of the comfort that only a handmade quilt can bring. 🟤

—David Jones, MFA,
   and Lisa Jones, BFA

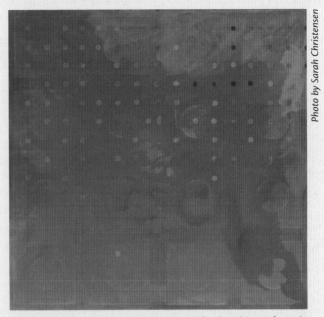

Photo by Sarah Christensen

Orange: Sibling Series #7, 53″ × 53″, painting by David Jones from the collection of BYU-Idaho

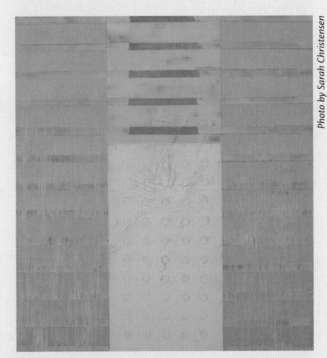

Photo by Sarah Christensen

Yellow Stripes: Sibling Series #5, 51″ × 53″, painting by David Jones from the collection of BYU-Idaho

QUILTING MAKES THE QUILT

The stitches that hold a quilt together can vary from minimalist to ornate. I've asked Angela Walters, a professional machine quilter, to share her thoughts about quilting on solids.

" While every quilt benefits from great quilting patterns, this is even more the case with modern quilts. The solid fabrics and large areas of negative space mean that the quilting is a more integral part of the quilt. In fact, it is another layer of art on the quilt. That definitely doesn't mean that the quilting needs to be hard or that it should overwhelm the quilt. It just means that the quilting needs to be carefully applied to bring out the most in your quilt top.

When you are deciding how to quilt, keep in mind the inspiration for the quilt itself. For instance, when I was quilting *City Rain*, knowing that it was designed with the thought of falling raindrops made picking out the quilting design easy. Large overlapping circles replicate the "ripple" effect of raindrops, allowing the quilting to bring the whole concept together. "

—Angela Walters

City Rain (full quilt on page 35)

A perfect example of the quilting doing the heavy lifting is *City Loft* (page 71). This "plain" two-color quilt speaks with the intricate Log Cabin–style quilting that Angela applied.

City Loft (full quilt on page 71)

THE CITY CHALLENGE

In a constant desire to expand my design skills, I give myself design challenges. Sometimes it's something minor, like using a particular fabric. At other times it might mean limiting myself as to how many colors I can use in a particular quilt (so hard). All of these challenges work to expand my abilities and creativity, and push me out of my comfort zone.

Knowing the city of Houston and its various neighborhoods gives me the sense that I could create Houston quilts forever and never run out of inspiration. Ah, but what about life outside of Houston, what about a city I've never been to, a place I'm not familiar with? In an effort to honor my children as well as challenge myself to create quilts that represent unfamiliar places, the "City Challenge" was born.

Here are the criteria and the "rules" I gave myself.

The Criteria

I asked each of my children to pick a city that was meaningful to him or her. There was some discussion regarding cities in this country versus international cities, but in the end we stuck with the United States. I asked them to tell me what was special to them about their city, specifics such as colors, smells, history—anything that would give me a sense of the place.

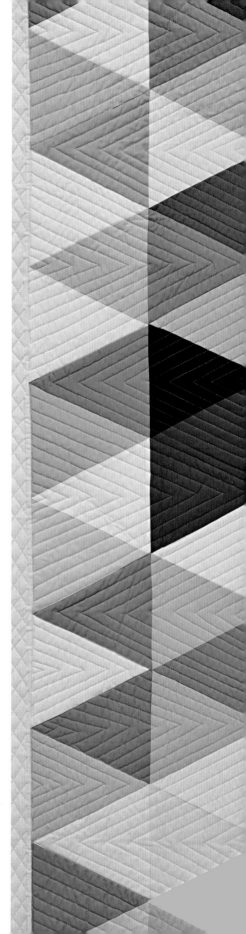

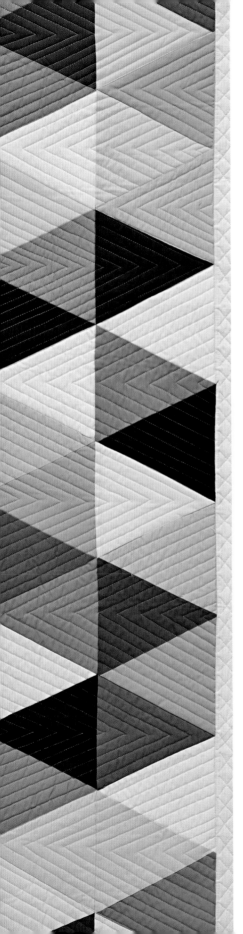

This was all done by email, and the responses ranged from a single sentence, providing little information to go on, to a several-sentence explanation about why a particular city was meaningful in that person's life. Where the descriptions were lacking, I searched for images on the Internet to give myself a place to start.

My challenge was to create quilts that were reflective of the chosen cities, incorporating the moods revealed in the brief descriptions provided by my children.

The Inspiration

This was truly a challenge; out of the four cities, I had visited only one, and that visit was brief—not much more than a plane stopover. All the cities were different, and the reasons for their importance in my children's lives were completely different as well.

Lizzy choose Portland, Oregon, for the seventeen bridges that span that city. Luke picked Fairfax, Virginia, for its beautiful green parks. Melissa chose Boston, Massachusetts, for the historical walking trail that goes through the city. Ashlee decided on Seattle, Washington, because she loves the constant rain and the beauty it creates.

The resulting quilts—the first four projects of this book—are abstracted perspectives representing four different points of view.

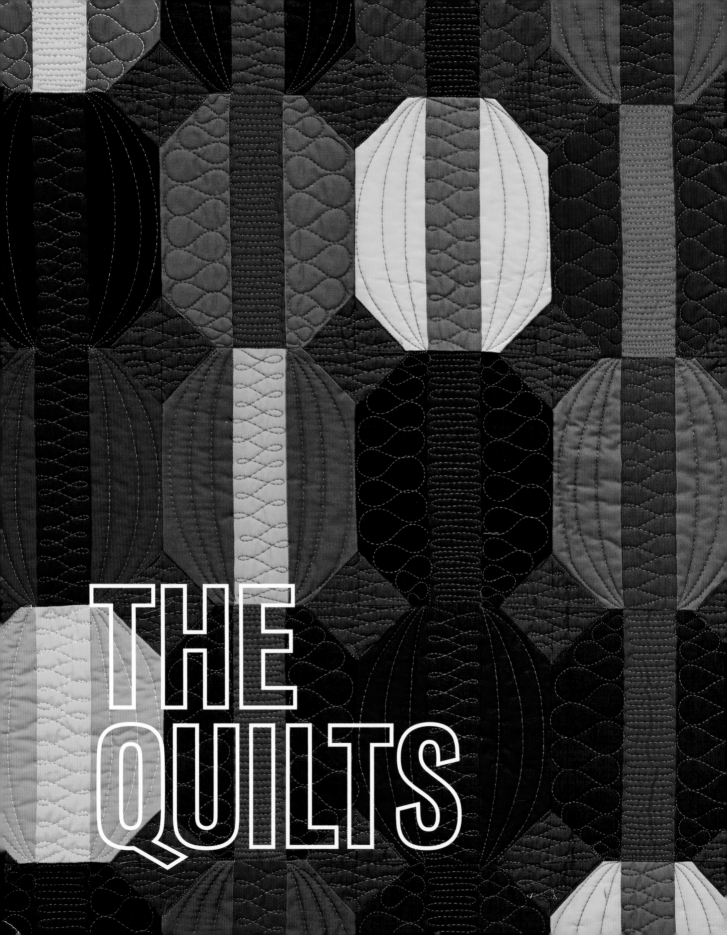

THE
QUILTS

The twelve quilt projects in this section are my interpretations of twelve different urban views. The first four—which resulted from the "City Challenge" (page 30)—represent Seattle, Boston, Portland, and Fairfax. The rest of these quilts reflect the way I see my home city of Houston—but they may be just as evocative of another city for you!

This quilt was inspired by the Emerald City of Seattle. Having spent a considerable amount of time in this city, I have vivid memories of walking around the rainy streets with people I love. With all of that rain, the streets can become dark and reflective surfaces where light and colors play in patterns. It's an ever-changing watercolor canvas.

—Ashlee House

CITY RAIN

FINISHED BLOCK: 1½″ × 1½″ | **FINISHED QUILT:** 80″ × 80″

Machine pieced by Cherri House and machine quilted by Angela Walters

Materials

Yardage is based on 42"-wide fabric.

Refer to my color list for City Rain *(page 108).*

- 5½ yards of dark gray fabric for blocks, borders, and binding

- 1 yard total of fabric in a variety of colors (this is a great opportunity to use up scraps from other quilt projects for blocks)

- 7½ yards of fabric for backing

- 88" × 88" piece of batting

TIP *This quilt is improvisational and could be considered a scrap quilt. When you have extra fabric from other projects, cut a 2" strip to set aside for use in a quilt such as* City Rain.

Cutting Instructions

From the dark gray fabric

Cut the pieces in the order listed:

- Cut 9 strips 2¼" × width of fabric.

- Cut 18 strips 2" × width of fabric; subcut into 2" × 2" squares (you need approximately 350 squares).

- Cut 4 strips 1½" × width of fabric. Subcut into 2 strips 40" long and 2 strips 38" long.

- Divide the remainder of the dark gray fabric lengthwise into 2 equal-size strips; subcut each strip into the following:

  1 piece 20½" × 40"

  1 piece 20½" × 80"

From the variously colored fabrics

- Cut 2" × 2" squares to make a total of approximately 280 squares.

QUILT CONSTRUCTION

1. Stitch the dark gray and colored 2″ × 2″ squares into 5-square strips; then join 5 of these sets to create a single row of 25 squares. Use your discretion as to the variety, quantity, and placement of colors throughout the quilt top. My rows varied from 2 colored squares in a row all the way to 18 colored squares in a row. Create a total of 25 rows of 25 squares. You will have some extra squares.

Make 25 rows, varying color placement.

2. Referring to the quilt diagram (page 38), lay out the 25 rows in an arrangement that you like. Sew the rows together and press, alternating the pressing direction of the seams between rows.

3. For the inner border, sew a 1½″ × 38″ dark gray strip to each side of the completed quilt center; press the seams away from the center. Then sew the 1½″ × 40″ strips to the top and bottom edges; press the seams away from the center.

4. Sew the 20½″ × 40″ outer border strips to the left and right sides; press. Stitch the 20½″ × 80″ outer border strips to the top and bottom quilt edges; press.

TIP *The length of the outer border strips makes them somewhat unwieldy, so for the sake of accuracy I recommend that you pin them in place before you stitch them to the quilt top. Match up the ends of the strips to the quilt corners and the centers of the strips to the quilt center. Then pin all along the entire length.*

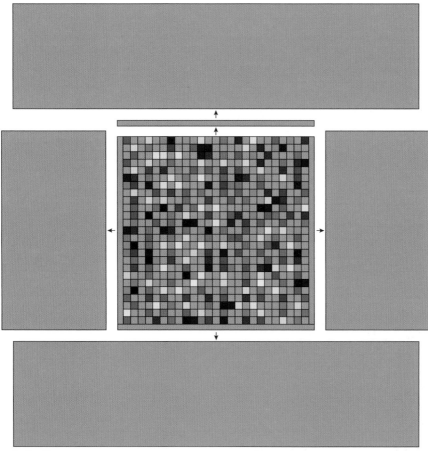

Quilt diagram

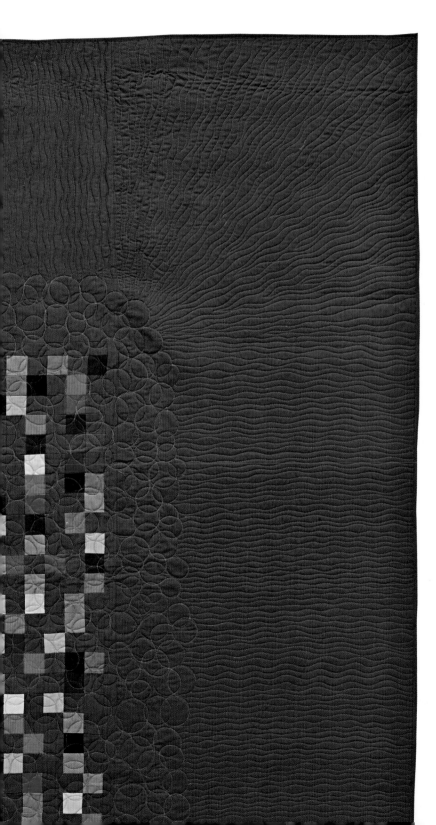

FINISHING

Refer to Finishing Basics (page 104) for information on layering, quilting, and binding the quilt. Use the dark gray 2¼″ strips for the binding.

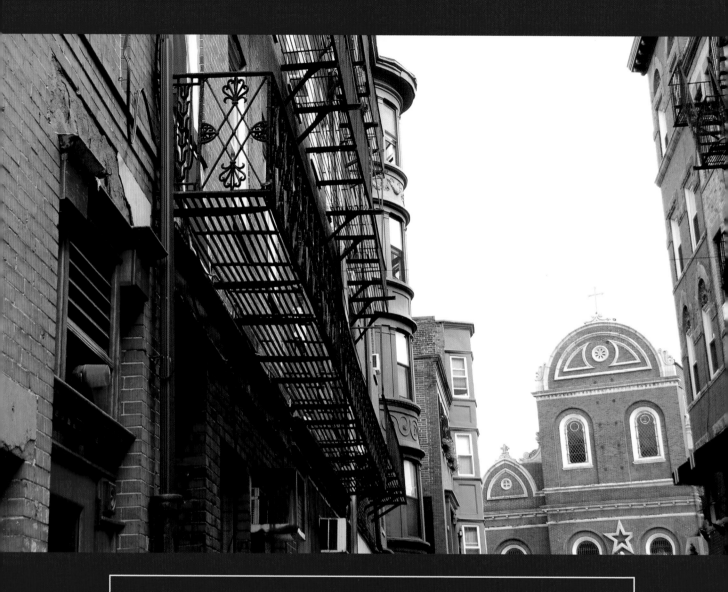

This quilt is inspired by the Freedom Trail in Boston, Massachusetts. I love the history that is part of the trail and this wonderful city. The vivid colors found in the quilt echo the colors of the trail. My time in Boston has great meaning to me and represents a turning point in my life. It was during this time that I chose what I wanted my life to be and the path that I would need to take to have that life. I see those choices in the Freedom Trail, and that is why I love this city.

—Melissa House

CITY TRAIL

FINISHED BLOCK: 6″ × 9″ | **FINISHED QUILT:** 66″ × 63″

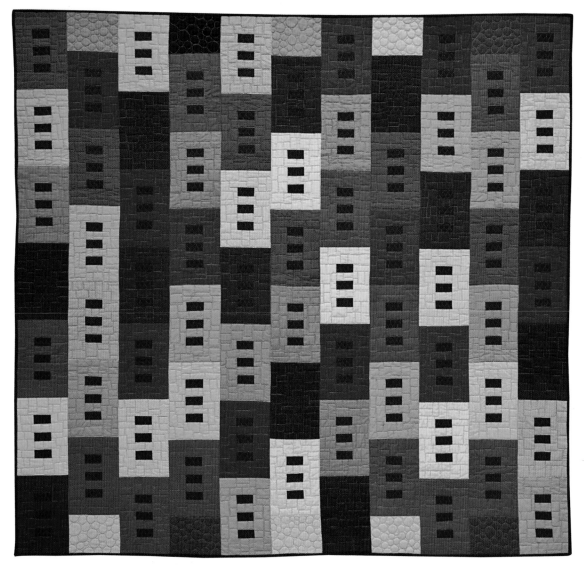

Machine pieced by Cherri House and machine quilted by Angela Walters

Materials

Yardage is based on 42˝-wide fabric.

*The project quilt has more than
12 colors, but for simplicity's sake
these instructions limit it to 12 fabrics.
Refer to my color list for* City Trail
(page 108).

- 1½ yards brick-colored fabric for
  blocks and binding

- 12 half-yard cuts of assorted
  fabrics in fall colors for blocks

- 4 yards of fabric for backing

- 71˝ × 74˝ piece of batting

Cutting Instructions

From the brick-colored fabric

- Cut 7 strips 2¼˝ × width of fabric.

- Cut 18 strips 1½˝ × width of fabric;
  cut in half lengthwise.

From the assorted half-yard fabrics

- From each fabric, cut 4 strips
  2½˝ × width of fabric; subcut
  2 strips of each fabric into
  2½˝ × 5½˝ pieces and the other
  2 strips of each fabric into
  2½˝ × 6½˝ pieces (you need
  12 pieces of each size from
  each fabric).

- From each fabric, cut 1 strip
  1½˝ × width of fabric; cut in half
  lengthwise.

- From 10 of the fabrics, cut 1 piece
  5˝ × 6½˝.

BLOCK ASSEMBLY

1. Sew 1½˝ × 21˝ strips to create a strip set for each color—2 strips of the same color and 3 brick-colored strips, as shown. Then cut 6 sections from each strip set, 2½˝ each. You need 6 sections of each color.

2½˝

Make 12, a strip set of each color.

2. Sew a 2½˝ × 5½˝ piece of the matching color to each side of a pieced strip unit. Press the seams away from the center unit. Then sew a 2½˝ × 6½˝ piece of that color to the top and bottom of the block; press away from the center as shown.

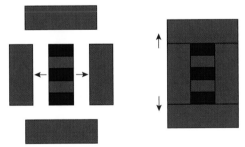

3. Repeat for all the pieced strip units to make a total of 72 blocks, 6 of each color.

QUILT CONSTRUCTION

1. Arrange the blocks on a flat design surface or design wall according to the quilt diagram, adding a 5″ × 6½″ piece at the top and bottom of each even-numbered column. Strive for a balance of color across the quilt.

2. Sew 7 blocks together end to end for columns 1, 3, 5, 7, 9, and 11; press.

3. Sew 6 blocks together with the border pieces for the remaining columns; press.

4. Join the columns to complete the quilt top; press.

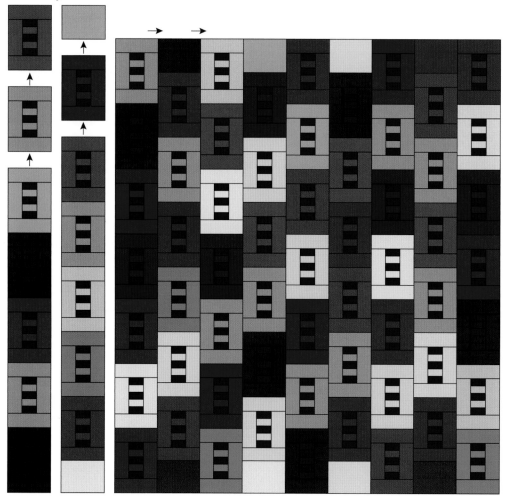

Quilt diagram

FINISHING

Refer to Finishing Basics (page 104) for information on layering, quilting, and binding the quilt. Use the brick-colored 2¼˝ strips for the binding.

On a whim I decided to move to Portland, Oregon, for a short time in 2009, because I had briefly visited in the early summer of 2008 and had of course fallen in love. I had not fallen in love with how extremely cool it was, or the food trucks, or the cyclists, or Voodoo Doughnuts. I had fallen in love with a tiny city, a big bookstore, and the fact that I was surrounded by water and trees almost anywhere I went. Everything was so green, almost like the trees were vibrating. When I did move there, I then quickly fell in love with New Seasons Market, roses, the MAX Light Rail system, and lots of other things that will always have a special place in my heart.

When you come into the city, all you see are bridges. This quilt speaks to the city's seventeen bridges. Most are beautiful, some are boring. Sometimes you get stuck on one, but all are functional. Kind of like a quilt, if you ask me.

—Elizabeth House

CITY BRIDGE

FINISHED BLOCK: 1½″ × 3″ | **FINISHED QUILT:** 50″ × 51″

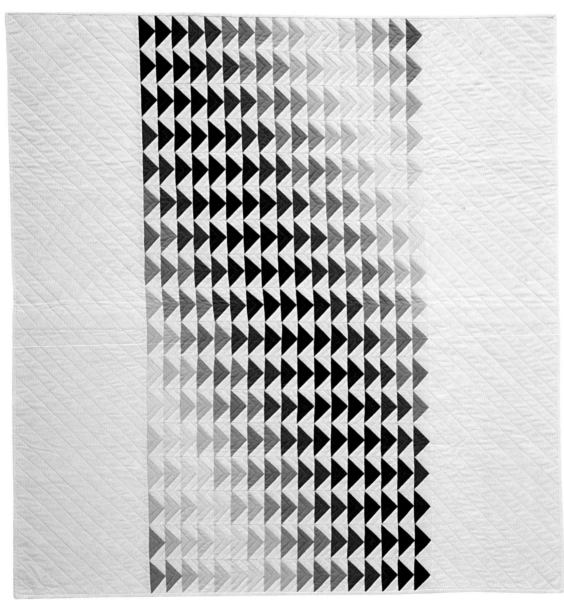

Machine pieced by Cherri House and machine quilted by Angela Walters

Materials

Yardage is based on 42˝-wide fabric.

As shown, City Bridge *was made with the colors listed below. All are solid fabrics by Robert Kaufman.*

- 3⅜ yards of white fabric for blocks, borders, and binding

- ¼ yard *each* of 11 solid-color fabrics: Black, Pepper, Charcoal, Coal, Slate, Medium Gray, Gray, Light Gray, Ash, Natural, and Bone

- ⅛ yard *each* of 12 solid-color fabrics: Pale Mint, Honey Dew, Pear, Pistachio, Sour Apple, Kiwi, Sky, Blue, Lake, Cornflower, Blue Jay, and Denim

- 3½ yards of fabric for backing

- 58˝ × 59˝ piece of batting

Cutting Instructions

From the white fabric

Cut in the following order:

- Cut 3 strips 12½˝ × width of fabric.

- Cut 6 strips 2¼˝ × width of fabric.

- Cut 29 strips 2˝ × width of fabric; subcut into 2˝ × 2˝ squares (you need 578 squares).

From the remaining fabrics

- Cut 2˝ strips × width of fabric; subcut 2˝ × 3½˝ pieces. Refer to the Flying Geese chart to find the number of pieces for each color. Mark each piece with the color number to assist you in assembling the quilt center.

TIP *To keep all the different-colored pieces organized, place them in zip-top plastic bags labeled with the color number.*

City Bridge Flying Geese

COLOR	NUMBER OF PIECES	COLOR	NUMBER OF PIECES	COLOR	NUMBER OF PIECES
Black #1	17	Ash #9	18	Kiwi #17	1
Pepper #2	32	Natural #10	16	Sky #18	6
Charcoal #3	30	Bone #11	14	Blue #19	5
Coal #4	28	Pale Mint #12	6	Lake #20	4
Slate #5	26	Honey Dew #13	5	Cornflower #21	3
Medium Gray #6	24	Pear #14	4	Blue Jay #22	2
Gray #7	22	Pistachio #15	3	Denim #23	1
Light Gray #8	20	Sour Apple #16	2		

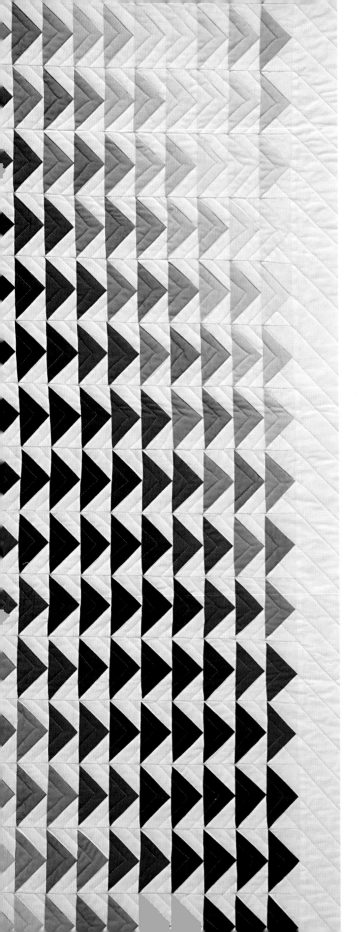

BLOCK ASSEMBLY

The quilt top is made up of Flying Geese blocks in understated colors that subtly transition outward to opposite corners.

1. Lightly draw a diagonal line on the back of all the white squares. With right sides together, place a white 2″ × 2″ square on an end of a 2″ × 3½″ color rectangle as shown. Sew on the diagonal from corner to corner, trim the seam allowance to ¼″, and press open.

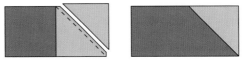

2. Next place another white 2″ × 2″ square on the other end of the rectangle. As before, sew on the diagonal from corner to corner, trim ¼″ from the stitching, and press open.

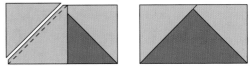

3. Referring to the chart, make the indicated number of Flying Geese blocks for each fabric color. Return the pieced units to the color-coded zip-top bags. When all the blocks are complete, you will have a total of 289 Flying Geese.

QUILT ASSEMBLY

1. Use a design wall or other flat surface to lay out the quilt center. Referring to the quilt diagram, arrange the Flying Geese as shown into rows with 17 blocks across and 17 rows down. Follow the numbering indicated in the diagram for the color placement of the blocks.

2. When you have the correct arrangement, pin and stitch each row using a precise ¼˝ seam to maintain the points. Press the seams carefully in alternate directions from row to row. Then join the rows together and press.

3. To make the borders, join the 3 white 12½˝ strips end to end; subcut into 2 strips 12½˝ × 51½˝. Sew the strips to the left and right sides of the quilt top. Press the seam allowances toward the borders.

Quilt diagram

FINISHING

Refer to Finishing Basics
(page 104) for information on
layering, quilting, and binding
the quilt. Use the white
2¼˝ strips for the binding.

This quilt is inspired by one of my favorite cities—
Fairfax, Virginia. Just an hour away from our nation's
capital, it is one of the most beautiful places I have
ever been. The colors and trees give a much-needed
sense of comfort and reverence to one of the busiest
and most hectic places on the planet.

—Luke House

CITY WOODS

FINISHED BLOCK: 7½″ × 7½″ | **FINISHED QUILT:** 60″ × 60″

Machine pieced by Cherri House and machine quilted by Angela Walters

Materials

Yardage is based on 42"-wide fabric.

Refer to my color list for City Woods *(page 108).*

- 3 yards of assorted green fabrics for the blocks

- 3 yards of assorted brown and tan fabrics for the block centers

- ½ yard of green fabric for binding

- 4 yards of fabric for backing

- 68" × 68" piece of batting

Cutting Instructions

From the assorted green fabrics
- Cut 64 squares 8" × 8".

From the browns and tans
- Cut 64 squares 7" × 7".

From the green binding fabric
- Cut 7 strips 2¼" × width of fabric.

BLOCK ASSEMBLY

You can create the circles in the *City Woods* blocks with traditional appliqué, fusible appliqué, raw-edge appliqué, or my favorite method— the 6-minute circle, created by Dale Fleming.

1. Gently fold the green 8″ × 8″ squares in half in both directions and crease the centers. The creases will serve as appliqué guidelines.

2. Create a 4″ finished circle. First draw your own 4″ circle template using a compass. Add a seam allowance if your chosen appliqué method requires it. Cut 64 circles from the 7″ × 7″ brown and tan squares.

3. Using your chosen appliqué method, apply the circle centers to the green background squares to complete the blocks. Make 64 blocks.

QUILT ASSEMBLY

1. On a flat design surface or design wall, lay out the blocks in an 8 × 8 arrangement.

2. When you are pleased with the arrangement, sew the blocks together in rows, and sew the rows together to complete the quilt top. Press the seams.

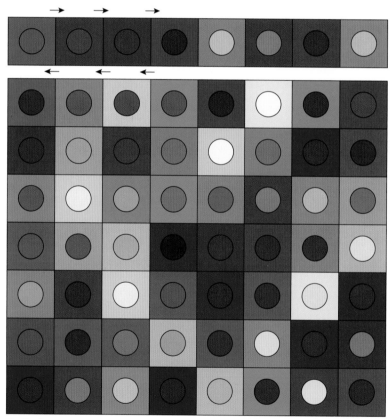

Quilt diagram

FINISHING

Refer to Finishing Basics (page 104) for information on layering, quilting, and binding the quilt. Use the green 2¼″ strips for the binding.

What two words do you frequently hear in reference to City Hall? Red tape! Though this design is seemingly simple, it's taken me four years to get the right balance of colors to create City Hall. First I added black, which didn't work; then I added white, and that didn't work. Anything other than the pure colors shown here made the quilt something less than it should be. Be sure to throw in some pops of orange and hot pink to create the depth and brilliance that these colors, playing together, can bring.

Improvisational design and grid work may not come to mind as a natural partnership, one being informal and the other very formal, but City Hall is exactly that. The improvisational part comes from the varying row widths and the varying fabric lengths within each row.

CITY HALL

FINISHED QUILT: 69″ × 74″

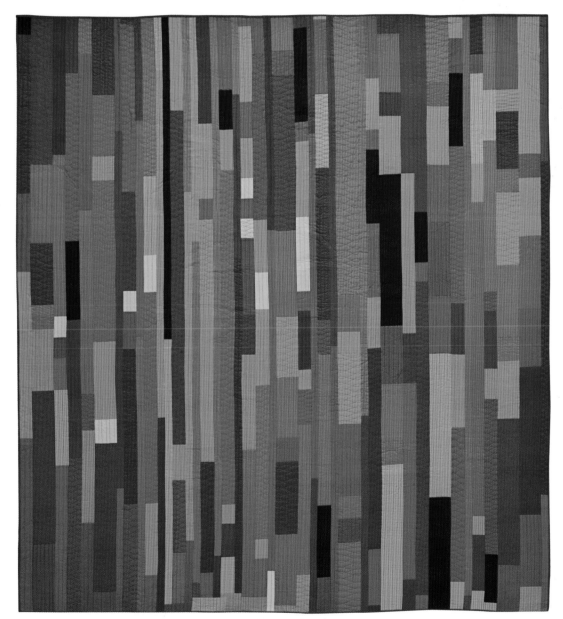

Machine pieced by Cherri House and machine quilted by Angela Walters

Materials

Yardage is based on 42˝-wide fabric.

Refer to my color list for City Hall *(page 108).*

- ½ yard each of 14 assorted red fabrics (carnation, hot pinks, burnt oranges)

- ⅝ yard of red fabric for binding

- 4½ yards of fabric for backing

- 77˝ × 82˝ piece of batting

Cutting Instructions

From each ½-yard length of assorted red fabrics

- Cut 1 strip 4˝ × width of fabric.

- Cut 2 strips 3˝ × width of fabric.

- Cut 1 strip 2˝ × width of fabric.

- Cut 1 strip 5˝ × width of fabric.

Subcut each strip as follows:

> 1 strip 20˝ long
>
> 1 strip 10˝ long
>
> 1 strip 5˝ long
>
> 1 strip 2½˝ long

Put all same-width strips into a single group or pile, regardless of color.

From the red binding fabric

- Cut 8 strips 2¼˝ × width of fabric.

QUILT CONSTRUCTION

1. Referring to Creating Strips with Solids (page 22), begin sewing same-width strips together end to end; press at each seam. Resulting strips will end up being different lengths, but make each at least 82″ long. Each of these long strips is a strip set. At this point, don't try to make everything even— that will be accomplished during the quilt assembly process.

2. Refer to the project photo (page 59) as you sew all the strip sets together. Align the strips as carefully as you can at the top in order to make an even edge; the bottom edge can be uneven, but both the top and the bottom can be trimmed evenly after all the strip sets are joined. Lay out the quilt top on a flat surface, measure the shortest strip, and trim everything to that length to even up the top and bottom edges. Square up the quilt top as you trim.

FINISHING

Refer to Finishing Basics (page 104) for information on layering, quilting, and binding the quilt. Use the red 2¼″ strips for the binding.

Ask any Houstonian what a freeway looks like in evening rush hour traffic during a deluge, and City Traffic *might describe it well. Everything comes to a grinding stop while drivers wait for what seem like endless buckets of rain to go away.*

Bright pops of color scattered across the quilt give variety and vibrancy as they transition from dark to light.

CITY TRAFFIC

FINISHED BLOCK: 1½″ × 7″ | **FINISHED QUILT:** 63″ × 77″

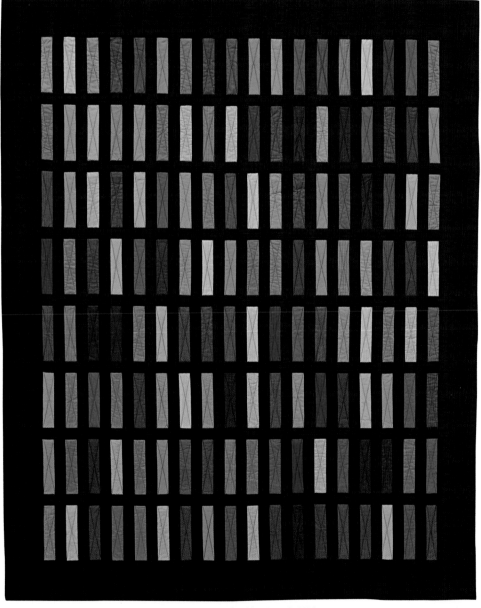

Machine pieced by Cherri House and machine quilted by Angela Walters

Materials

Yardage is based on 42″-wide fabric.

Refer to my color list for City Traffic *(page 108).*

- 4 yards of black fabric for background and binding

- 2 yards of assorted green, blue, and purple fabrics

- 5 yards of fabric for backing

- 71″ × 85″ piece of batting

Cutting Instructions

From the black fabric

Cut in the following order:

- Cut 10 strips 2″ × width of fabric.

- Cut 28 more strips 2″ × width of fabric; subcut into 7½″ strips (you need 136 pieces).

- Cut 7 strips 5½″ × width of fabric.

- Cut 8 strips 2¼″ × width of fabric.

From the blue, green, and purple fabrics

- Cut strips 2″ × width of fabric; subcut into 7½″ strips, to make a total of 144 units. Reserve 8 strips that include 8 different colors and set these reserved strips aside until later. (If using scraps rather than yardage, simply cut out 2″ × 7½″ pieces from the scraps.)

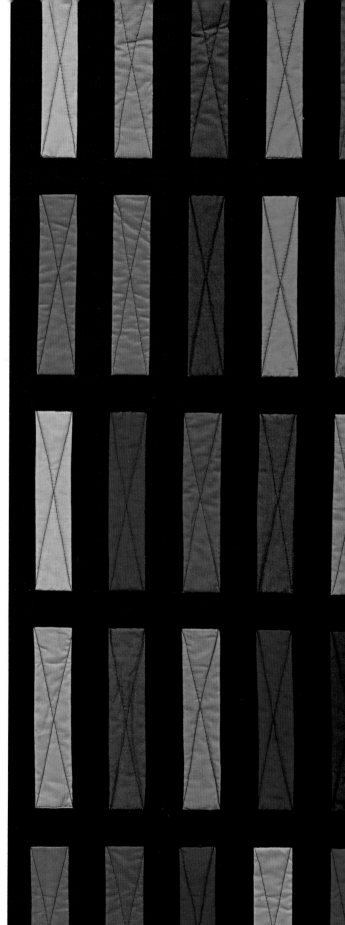

ROW ASSEMBLY

1. Sew together the 10 black strips (2″ × width of fabric), end to end; subcut into 7 strips 2″ × 53″. This will be the sashing between the rows.

2. Sew together a 2″ × 7½″ color strip and a 2″ × 7½″ black strip along a long edge. Repeat to make a total of 136 sewn pairs.

3. Refer to the quilt diagram. Sew together 17 pairs to make a row. Complete the row by adding a color 2″ × 7½″ strip from the reserved set. Repeat to make a total of 8 rows.

QUILT CONSTRUCTION

1. Join the 7 black strips (5½″ × width of fabric) end to end. Subcut into 2 border strips 5½″ × 53″ long and 2 border strips 5½″ × 77″ long.

2. Sew a 5½″ × 53″ black border strip to the top edge of the first row of blocks. Press the seam allowance toward the border strip.

3. For rows 2 through 8, sew a 2″ × 53″ black sashing strip to the top of each row; press toward the sashing strip. Repeat to sew all the rows together as you work your way down the quilt top.

4. Sew the remaining 5½″ × 53″ black border strip to the bottom of the final row; press toward the border.

5. Sew a 5½″ × 77″ black border strip to each side of the quilt top.

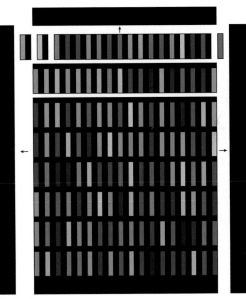

Quilt diagram

FINISHING

Refer to Finishing Basics (page 104) for information on layering, quilting, and binding the quilt. Use the black 2¼″ strips for the binding.

Strange but true ... on a rare occasion, maybe once or twice a year, the weather in Houston over the course of a single day will be so varied that you can actually see all of the colors represented in City Sky. *The best skies seem to be after a late-afternoon thunderstorm, and the colors of the sunset then are like cotton candy. Those are my favorites!*

While simple in piecing, City Sky *is all about the color placement and precise sewing. The goal is have the colors of the sky look seamless.*

CITY SKY

FINISHED BLOCK: 10″ × 20″ | **FINISHED QUILT:** 80″ × 60″

Machine pieced by Cherri House and machine quilted by Angela Walters

Materials

Yardage is based on 42˝-wide fabric.

Refer to my color list for City Sky (page 109).

- 24 fat quarters (18˝ × 22˝) in assorted "sky" colors

- ⅝ yard of fabric for binding (I used navy)

- 5 yards of fabric for backing

- 68˝ × 88˝ piece of batting

Cutting Instructions

From each fat quarter
- Cut 8 strips 1¾˝ × 20½˝; sort by color.

From the binding fabric
- Cut 8 strips 2¼˝ × width of fabric.

BLOCK ASSEMBLY

Each "block" consists of 8 strips, either light/medium or medium/dark. The illusion of larger and smaller blocks is created by extending the color sequence of a block into an adjacent block (above or below). You can see this happen in (A) the far left column of the quilt in the bottom 2 blocks (block 6 extends *up* into block 5). Study the quilt photo and you can see this happen again in (B) the top 2 blocks of the far right column (block 1 extends *down* into block 2). Can you find it happening again in another place? Hint: (C) Column 2, block 3 extends down into block 4.

1. Using a flat design surface or a design wall, arrange the strips to create 24 blocks in 4 columns of 6 blocks each, referring to the quilt diagram (page 69). Decide in which blocks you want to continue the color sequence and arrange the strips accordingly. Play with the arrangement until you are pleased. Cut additional 1¾˝ × 20½˝ strips if necessary.

2. Stitch together 8 strips to make each block. Working from left to right, press the block seam allowances in alternating directions (rows 1 and 3 downward, rows 2 and 4 upward, and so on).

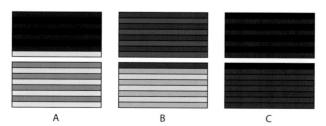

A   B   C

3. Join all the blocks in each vertical column, and then sew together the 4 columns.

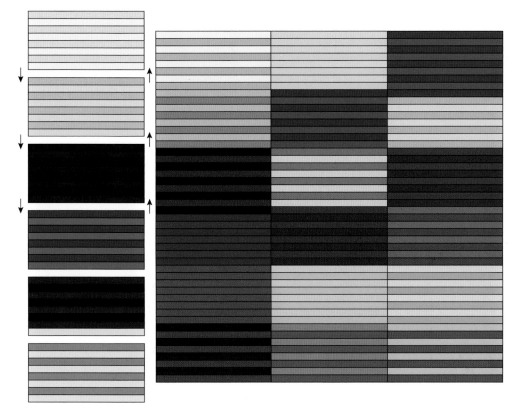

Quilt diagram

TIP *I definitely recommend that you pin the blocks before sewing them together—precise stitching is critical to achieve a seamless effect of colors flowing one into the other.*

FINISHING

Refer to Finishing Basics (page 104) for information on layering, quilting, and binding the quilt. Use the 2¼˝ strips for the binding.

I love the building that inspired this quilt! It sits across the street from City Hall in Houston. The red-trimmed windows charm me every time I see them.

I made the quilt using Essex Linen from Robert Kaufman, a linen/cotton blend. A snow- or off-white solid would work as a perfect alternative fabric.

CITY LOFT

FINISHED BLOCK: 6″ × 6″ | **FINISHED QUILT:** 74″ × 74″

Machine pieced by Cherri House and machine quilted by Angela Walters

Materials

Yardage is based on 42˝-wide fabric.

Refer to my color list for City Loft *(page 109).*

- 5 yards of Robert Kaufman Essex Linen or other white or off-white fabric

- 1¾ yards of red fabric for the blocks and binding

- 4⅝ yards of fabric for backing

- 82˝ × 82˝ piece of batting

TIP *When you are working with a heavier fabric such as a linen/cotton blend, increase the stitch length to achieve a smooth stitching line.*

Cutting Instructions

From the white fabric

- Cut 7 strips 6½˝ × width of fabric; subcut into 6½˝ × 4½˝ pieces (you need 56).

- Cut 7 strips 5½˝ × width of fabric; subcut into 5½˝ × 5½˝ squares (you need 49).

- Cut 16 strips 4½˝ × width of fabric.

From the red fabric

- Cut 3 strips 6½˝ × width of fabric; subcut into 98 strips 1˝ × 6½˝.

- Cut 3 strips 5½˝ × width of fabric; subcut into 98 strips 1˝ × 5½˝.

- Cut 8 strips 2¼˝ × width of fabric.

BLOCK ASSEMBLY

1. Sew a 1˝ × 5½˝ red strip to the left and right side of a 5½˝ × 5½˝ white square; press the seam allowance toward the red strip.

2. Sew a 1˝ × 6½˝ red strip to the top and bottom of the white square; press toward the red strip.

3. Repeat to make a total of 49 blocks.

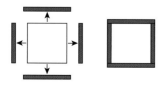

QUILT CONSTRUCTION

1. Refer to the quilt diagram (page 73) to make the columns. For each column sew 8 white 4½˝ × 6½˝ pieces alternating with 7 quilt blocks. Press the seams toward the red strips.

2. Repeat to make a total of 7 columns.

3. For the sashing strips between the rows, sew pairs of 4½˝ × width of fabric white strips together end to end to make a total of 8 strip sets. Cut 8 sashing strips 4½˝ × 74½˝.

4. Sew the quilt top together by alternating sashing columns and pieced block columns, starting and ending with a sashing column.

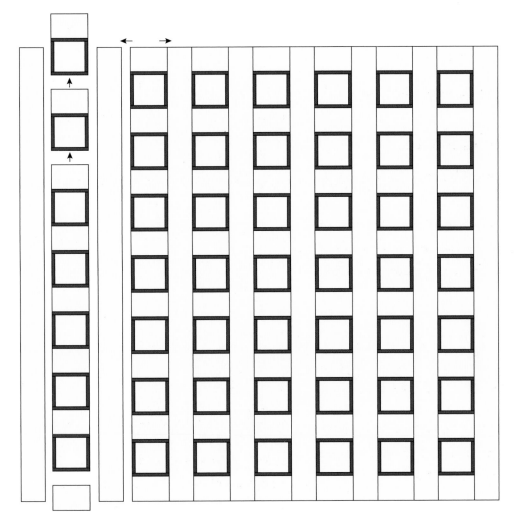

Quilt diagram

FINISHING

Refer to Finishing Basics (page 104) for information on layering, quilting, and binding the quilt. Use the red 2¼˝ strips for the binding.

About two years ago I discovered Mountain Valley Spring Water—little green glass bottles of sparkling bliss delivered to my house every Thursday. The only downfall: What to do with all those glass bottles? A recycling center that took glass solved the problem—and what a variety of color is to be found there!

In this quilt, the traditional Snowball block becomes a modern classic.

CITY RECYCLING

FINISHED BLOCK: 10½″ × 10½″ | **FINISHED QUILT:** 63″ × 63″

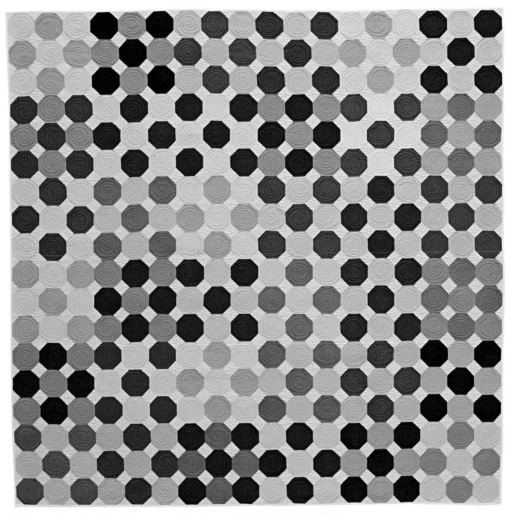

Machine pieced by Cherri House and machine quilted by Angela Walters

Materials

Yardage is based on 42˝-wide fabric.

Refer to my color list for City Recycling *(page 109).*

- 2¾ yards of off-white fabric for the background and binding

- 5 yards of assorted green, blue, tan, yellow, and red fabrics (I used ⅛ yard each of 36 colors in my quilt)

- 4 yards of fabric for quilt backing

- 71˝ × 71˝ piece of batting

Cutting Instructions

From the off-white fabric

- Cut 7 strips 2¼˝ × width of fabric.

- Cut 50 strips 1½˝ × width of fabric; subcut into 1½˝ × 1½˝ squares for a total of 1,296 squares.

From the assorted fabrics

- From each color, cut 1 strip 4˝ × width of fabric; subcut into 4˝ × 4˝ squares (9 of each color). You need a total of 324 squares. Keep the different colors separated.

Cutting Corners

One of my favorite traditional blocks is the Snowball block. The corners appear to be triangles, and what was once an ordinary square block now becomes more special.

Nothing could be easier than creating a Snowball block. You start with a plain square block and place a smaller square on each corner, right sides together. Sew across the corner on the diagonal of the small square, trim ¼″ from the seam line, press outward toward the corner, and— ta-da—quilting magic!

I use this technique on rectangles, too— see *City Beat* (page 81).

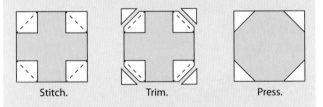

Stitch.   Trim.   Press.

BLOCK ASSEMBLY

1. Lightly draw a diagonal line from corner to corner on the back of all the 1½″ squares. Create 9 Snowball patches of each color (324 patches in all), as shown in Cutting Corners (at left), using all the off-white 1½″ squares and the colored 4″ squares.

2. Using a light color and a dark color combination for each block, arrange the patches into 18 light and 18 dark blocks of 9 Snowballs each. (Light blocks will have 5 light and 4 dark Snowball patches; dark blocks will have 5 dark and 4 light patches.) Sew each block, pinning to ensure precise seam intersections. Press.

Make 18 dark blocks.

Make 18 light blocks.

QUILT CONSTRUCTION

1. Alternate light and dark 9-patch blocks on a design wall or other flat surface to come up with a pleasing arrangement 6 blocks wide and 6 blocks long. Alternating light and dark blocks will create diagonal lines of dark patches, adding a secondary pattern to the quilt design.

2. Sew the units together by rows. Press the seam allowances open to reduce bulk.

3. Join the rows to complete the quilt top.

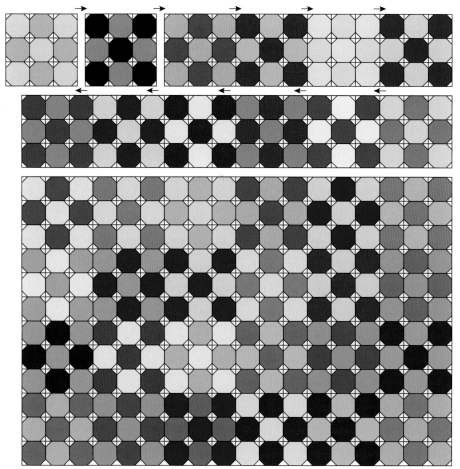

Quilt diagram

FINISHING

Refer to Finishing Basics (page 104) for information on layering, quilting, and binding the quilt. Use the off-white 2¼″ strips for the binding.

Would you believe me if I told you my favorite music is electronica? House, techno, ambient—I love them all! My daughter thought this quilt should be named City Jazz, since that's what the colors bring to mind for her. This quilt represents the nightlife of every city.

The bright pops of yellow and orange create a sense of light, warmth, and motion against the dark, cool background. Too many of these warm colors would overwhelm the quilt; a little goes a long way.

CITY BEAT

FINISHED BLOCK: 5½″ × 7″ | **FINISHED QUILT:** 66″ × 70″

Machine pieced by Cherri House and machine quilted by Angela Walters

Materials

Yardage is based on 42˝-wide fabric.

Refer to my color list for City Beat *(page 109).*

- 2 yards of charcoal gray fabric for the background and binding

- ¼ yard each of 24 different colors of fabric

- 4⅛ yards of fabric for backing

- 74˝ × 78˝ piece of batting

Cutting Instructions

From the charcoal gray fabric

- Cut 24 strips 2˝ × width of fabric; subcut into 2˝ × 2˝ squares (you need 480 squares).

- Cut 7 strips 2¼˝ × width of fabric.

From each of the 24 fabrics

- Cut 2 strips 2½˝ × width of fabric (keep paired).

- Cut 1 strip 2˝ × width of fabric.

BLOCK CONSTRUCTION

1. Create a strip set by sewing a 2″ × width of fabric strip (choose any color) between a matching pair of 2½″ × width of fabric strips (a different color). Press the seams open. Repeat to make a total of 24 strip sets. Subcut into 7½″ blocks; you need 120 blocks in all.

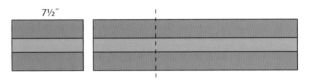

2. Refer to Cutting Corners (page 77). Draw a diagonal line from corner to corner on all the gray 2″ squares. With right sides facing, sew a 2″ × 2″ gray square onto each corner of a block from Step 1, stitching on the diagonal of each small square across the block corner. Trim ¼″ outside the stitched line; press back the corner. Repeat for all 120 blocks.

Make 120.

QUILT CONSTRUCTION

1. On a design surface, arrange the blocks in 10 rows of 12 blocks each. Distribute the colors to create the effect of pulsating lights. Sew the blocks into rows.

2. Stitch together the rows to complete the quilt top. Press the seams open.

Quilt diagram

FINISHING

Refer to Finishing Basics (page 104) for information on layering, quilting, and binding the quilt. Use the charcoal gray 2¼″ strips for the binding.

When my children were small, we would all lie on the bed together during a thunderstorm, staring out the window oohing and aahing as we watched for the biggest bolt of lightning. The negative space of the narrow vertical sashing in City Electric lets diagonal images crisscross this composition like lightning in a thunderstorm. Using a triangle ruler and fabric strips makes these columns

CITY ELECTRIC

FINISHED BLOCK HEIGHT: 6″ | **FINISHED QUILT:** 54″ × 60″

Machine pieced by Cherri House and machine quilted by Angela Walters

Materials

Yardage is based on 42˝-wide fabric.

Refer to my color list for City Electric (page 109).

- 1 yard of off-white fabric for sashing and binding

- 3¼ yards of assorted green, blue, gray, khaki, white, and tan fabrics for blocks

- 3½ yards of fabric for backing

- 62˝ × 68˝ piece of batting

- EZ Quilting by Wrights Tri-Recs Tools acrylic triangle ruler set (*optional*)

Cutting Instructions

Copy the City Electric template (page 91) at 100%, unless you are using a specialty triangle ruler. If using a specialty tool, follow the manufacturer's instructions to cut triangles the same size as the template pattern.

From the off-white fabric

- Cut 5 strips 2½˝ × width of fabric for sashing.

- Cut 6 strips 2¼˝ × width of fabric for binding.

From the green, blue, gray, khaki, and tan fabrics

- Cut 16 strips 6½˝ × width of fabric. Then cut triangles from the strips using the Tri Tool triangle ruler or template. (Place the ruler on the fabric strip with the top and bottom edges of the ruler on the edges of the fabric. Cut along the side edges of the ruler, rotate the ruler, and cut the next triangle.) You can cut 11 triangles per fabric strip; you need 168 triangles in all.

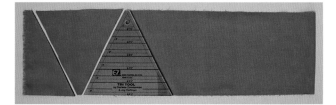

QUILT CONSTRUCTION

Often isosceles triangles are used to create stars within square blocks. We'll be using them to create bolts of lightning.

1. On a design wall or other flat surface, arrange 8 columns with 21 triangles in each column, referring to the quilt diagram (page 90). Scatter the colors across the quilt to create diagonal patterns that will give the effect of lightning shooting across the sky.

2. When you are pleased with the color placement, sew each column together. With the flat tips of the triangles positioned as shown (A), flip the triangle on the right on top of the triangle on the left with right sides together. Pin in place as shown (B). *Note how the flat tip of the top triangle aligns with the point of the triangle underneath.* As you sew the triangles together, it's important to use an exact ¼" seam allowance for matching points. Press the seam and add additional triangles to complete the column. Sew a total of 8 columns.

3. Refer to the quilt diagram (page 90). Sew the columns into pairs with the flat triangle bases facing together as shown. Place a pin through each intersection, column to column, to align the seams. Stitch an exact ¼" seam for precise points. Repeat to make 4 sections, each with 2 columns.

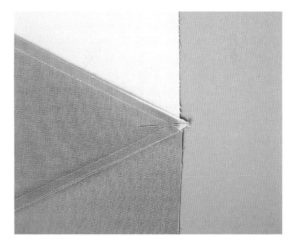

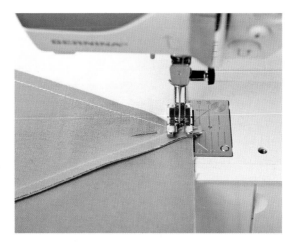

4. Before sewing the quilt together, you'll need to trim the top and bottom triangles in each 2-column section to straighten the edges. Place the end of a 2-column section on a flat work surface. Use a dot to mark the centers of the 2 end triangle bases of the column as shown. Lightly mark a line connecting the base center dots (the stitching line in the diagram). This line should pass through the intersection of the triangle points in the center seam and will be the stitching line when you add the binding. Measure ¼″ toward the outside of the stitching line and draw a line as shown. Cut on this line.

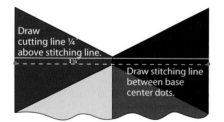

5. Sew the 2½″ off-white sashing strips together, end to end. Measure the length of the 2-column sections and cut 3 sashing strips to that length.

6. Sew the sashing strips between the 2-column sections to complete the quilt top.

Quilt diagram

FINISHING

Refer to Finishing Basics (page 104) for information on layering, quilting, and binding the quilt. Use the off-white 2¼″ strips for the binding.

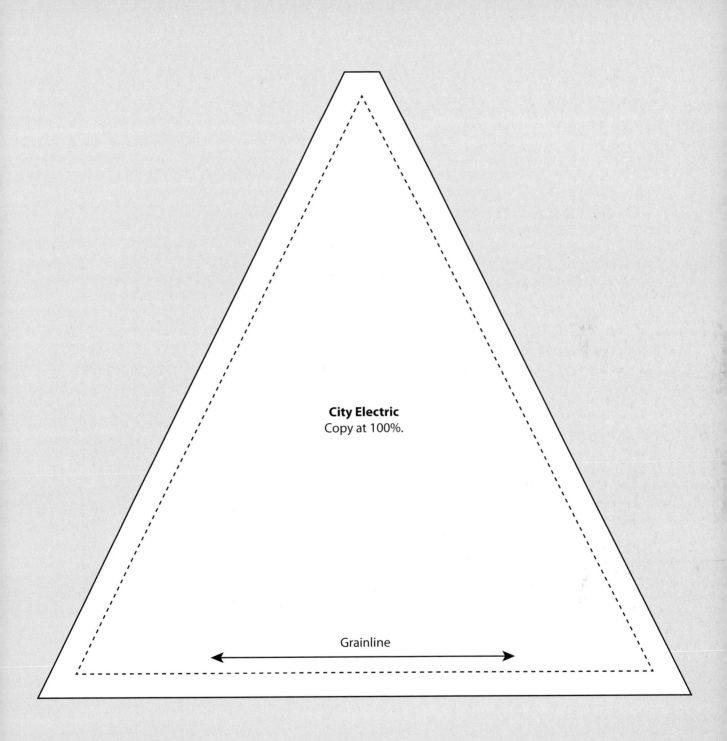

City Electric
Copy at 100%.

Grainline

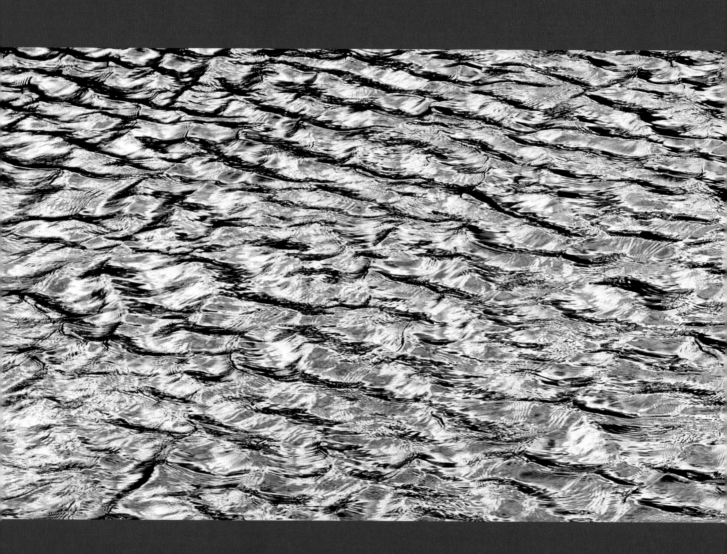

Once upon a time a silly woman tried to take a photo of a quilt and fell into a lake. How could I not make a quilt to honor my ridiculousness and survival? City Lake is created using a 60° ruler and fabric strips. The triangles are equilateral. This quilt would be a perfect opportunity to substitute batiks for solids, or use hand-dyes in a multitude of blues and greens.

CITY LAKE

FINISHED BLOCK HEIGHT: 4½″ | **FINISHED QUILT:** 76″ × 85″

Machine pieced by Cherri House and machine quilted by Angela Walters

Materials

Yardage is based on 42″-wide fabric.

Refer to my color list for City Lake (page 109).

- 1⅜ yards of black fabric for outside border and binding

- 7¾ yards of assorted blue, green, and purple fabrics for blocks (I slipped in an unexpected gold)

- 5¼ yards of fabric for backing

- 84″ × 93″ piece of batting

- Creative Grids Non-Slip Multi-Size 45°/60° Triangle ruler or other specialty ruler for equilateral triangles (*optional*)

Cutting Instructions

Copy the City Lake template (page 98) at 100%, unless you are using a specialty triangle ruler. If using a ruler, follow the manufacturer's instructions to cut triangles the same size as the template pattern.

From the black fabric

- Cut 8 strips 2½″ × width of fabric for border.

- Cut 9 strips 2¼″ × width of fabric for binding.

From the blue, green, and purple fabrics

- Cut 48 strips 5″ × width of fabric; subcut into 522 triangles, using a specialty 60° triangle ruler or the template. You can cut 11 triangles per fabric strip.

TIP *To use the Creative Grids Multi-Size 45°/60° Triangle ruler, place the 60° triangle section of the ruler on the fabric as shown and align the strip with the 5″ mark on the ruler. Cut along the side edges of the ruler. Then rotate the ruler to make the next cut.*

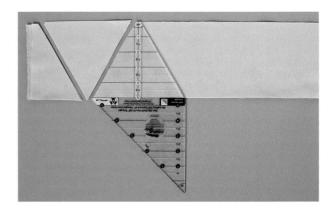

BLOCK ASSEMBLY

When considering color placement, think of a body of water with varying depths, with light shimmering on its surface. You can lay out the entire quilt to be sure of exact color placement before even sewing any units together, or you can sew the units together with random triangles and then play with the arrangement of the assembled blocks. Your choice!

1. With right sides facing up and with the flat tips of the triangles positioned as shown, flip the triangle on the right on top of the triangle on the left. With right sides together, sew the 2 triangles together using a precise ¼˝ seam, matching the corners as shown. Press the seam open.

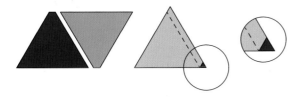

2. Add another triangle to create a 3-piece unit as shown. Press the seam open. You need 16 of these units. Set these aside for now.

3. To create a 4-piece block, repeat Steps 1 and 2 to make a 3-piece unit. Then sew a fourth triangle to the top of the 3-piece unit as shown. Press the seam open. Make 104 of the 4-piece blocks.

QUILT CONSTRUCTION

Before you sew the blocks together, you may want to arrange them on a design wall. If you want to assemble the quilt with random blocks, that's OK too.

1. Sew 13 of the 4-piece triangle units to form a row, with a 3-piece unit on each end as shown. Repeat to make a total of 8 rows. (The units are solid-colored in the diagram for easy identification.)

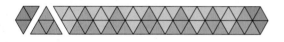

2. For the top and bottom rows, sew 29 triangles together as in Steps 1 and 2 in Block Assembly (page 95). Make 2 rows.

3. Sew together all the rows, pinning carefully at the seam intersections. Press the seams open. The edges of the quilt will be uneven.

4. To trim the quilt sides, lay the quilt top on a flat surface. Lightly mark a line through the triangle points (the stitching line in the diagram). This should be a straight line down the sides of the quilt. Measure ¼″ toward the outside of the stitching line, and cut along this line as shown.

Assembly diagram

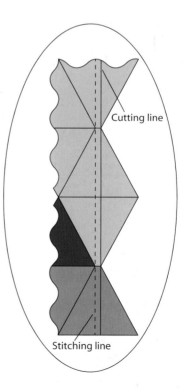

Cutting line

Stitching line

5. Sew together the black 2½″ border strips, and then subcut into 2 strips 2½″ × 81½″ and 2 strips 2½″ × 74¼″.

6. Sew the 81½″ strips to the left and right of the quilt top; press the seams toward the border. Attach the 74¼″ strips to the top and bottom of the quilt top; press toward the border.

Quilt diagram

FINISHING

Refer to Finishing Basics (page 104) for information on layering, quilting, and binding the quilt. Use the black 2¼″ strips for the binding.

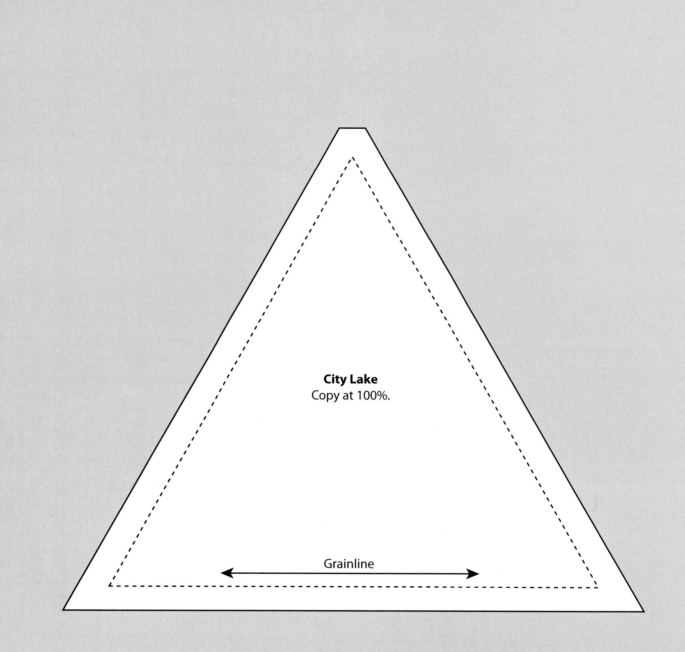

City Lake
Copy at 100%.

Grainline

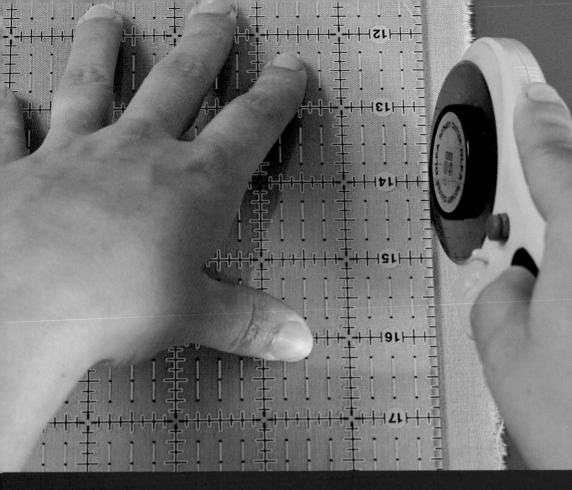

QUILTMAKING
ESSENTIALS

Correct construction and finishing are essential if you want your quilt to be a success. Here, I offer some of my tips and techniques, along with basic finishing methods. If you're a beginner or just want to refresh your skills, you may also want to consult a good general quilting book.

USEFUL TECHNIQUES

Whether you have a dedicated sewing studio or use your dining-room table as a work space, try to organize it for the steps you'll follow along the way to creating quilts. If at all possible, have a small ironing station close to your sewing machine for pressing seams during block construction. To make the most of your quilting time, it's also helpful to have rotary cutting supplies close by, so that you can make a seamless (pun intended!) transition back and forth between sewing and cutting or trimming.

PRESSING

Ironing and pressing are *two different operations. Ironing* means sliding the iron back and forth with gentle pressure to remove wrinkles from fabric. *Pressing* is setting the iron down on an area in order to set seams. To press long seams, slightly lift the iron, move it to the next section, and press in the new area.

Iron all of your fabric before cutting it. But during the block construction phase, avoid ironing and use careful pressing techniques instead.

Pressing instructions vary from pattern to pattern; follow the individual directions for each project. In general, press seams toward the darker fabric to prevent show-through from the light side of a quilt block, unless instructed to do otherwise. As you construct each block, press seams in opposing directions, so that when the units are sewn together, opposing seams will abut or nest. Seams that nest will require less pinning, cause less frustration, and result in flatter seams.

Press lightly, and avoid using a very hot iron or over-ironing, which can distort shapes and blocks. Be especially careful when pressing bias edges, which stretch easily. Always press from the front side of the block to prevent tucks in seams. Quilt row seams should be pressed in alternating directions from row to row so that the seams will nest.

Steam or no steam? It's really a matter of personal preference. A common practice among quilters is to use a dry iron during the block construction process and then use steam to set the block once it's complete.

Finger Pressing

During the block construction process, finger pressing is a good alternative to using the iron to press each individual seam.

To finger-press, use your index finger as an iron, applying gentle pressure along the length of the seam.

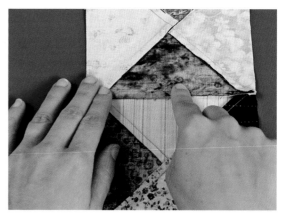

Finger pressing

ROTARY CUTTING

Here are some tips for proper rotary cutting:

- *Be very careful* when working with a rotary cutter—the blade is incredibly sharp! Dispose of dull blades safely.

- Always cut away from yourself.

- Attach sticky dots or sandpaper dots to the underside of the ruler to keep it from slipping when you are cutting.

- Where applicable, cut strips first and then subcut them into smaller units.

- To cut strips, fold the fabric from selvage to selvage so that both fabric layers are flat and are lined up evenly along the selvage edge. Place the fabric fold on the cutting mat grid line closest to you.

For an excellent guide to rotary cutting techniques, see Nancy Johnson-Srebro's *All-in-One Rotary Cutting Magic with Omnigrid*, available from C&T Publishing.

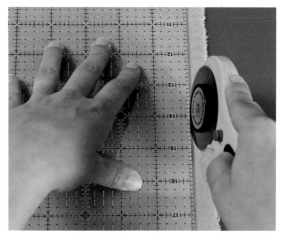

Correct rotary cutting technique

CONSTRUCTION

A ¼˝ seam allowance is standard for quilt construction, so you will need a ¼˝ quilter's presser foot for your sewing machine. Since accurate sewing is essential so that all of the pieced units fit together correctly, it's a good idea to do a test seam to check that the presser foot is accurate.

Cut two strips of fabric 3˝ × 4˝. Place them right sides together, slide them under the presser foot (aligned with the foot's edge), and sew the 4˝ length of the strips. Press the seam open.

The finished piece should measure 4˝ × 5½˝. If it doesn't, your ¼˝ foot is not an accurate guide. Instead, place a piece of electrical tape on the throat plate—either just inside the presser foot edge or just outside it, depending on whether your test came out too wide or too narrow. Repeat the test to ensure that your seam allowances are actually ¼˝.

There's no need to backstitch at the ends of seams. Seam lines will be crossed by other seams, which will anchor them in place.

Sewing over Seam Allowances

To ensure that seam allowances stay flat as you sew over them, use the point of a stiletto to hold them down as they approach the presser foot.

PINNING

I'm a firm believer in using pins while piecing! Buy long, super-thin pins specifically made for piecing. My favorites are Dritz Quilting Crystal Glass Head Pins.

The purposes of pinning are to match seams and to prevent shifting during sewing. If seams are pressed in alternate directions from row to row, the seams will nest when placed together. Pin at every intersection of seams and between intersections approximately every 1½″–2″. Insert the pin in the seam approximately ¼″ in from the raw edge; don't pin through the seam allowance. Check underneath to make sure the pin is entering the matching seam in the same spot.

For bulky seams where the seams are pressed open, insert the pin directly in the center of the seam on the top and bottom fabrics.

Don't sew over pins—doing so can really damage your sewing machine! Remove each pin just before it reaches the sewing needle.

Position pins this way.

FINISHING BASICS

You're almost there! But before you can snuggle up with your finished quilt or give it to a loved one, you need to layer the top with the backing and batting, baste everything in place, and then quilt and bind your creation.

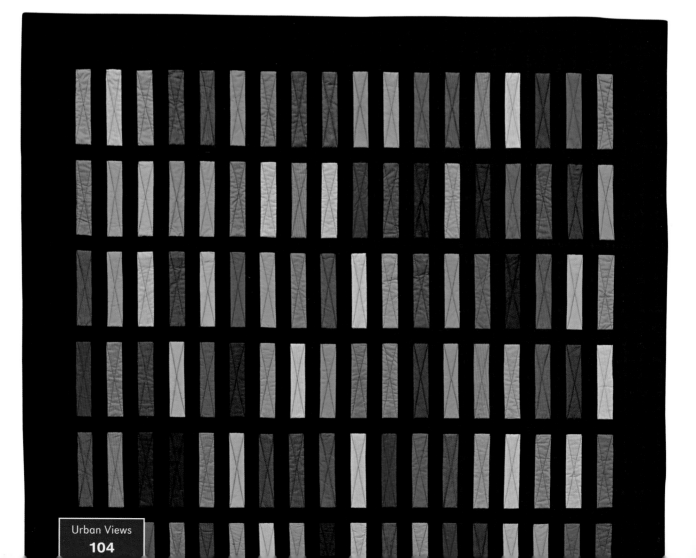

BORDERS

When border strips are cut on the crosswise grain, piece the strips together to achieve the needed lengths.

Squared Borders

In most cases the side borders are sewn on first. When you have finished the quilt top, measure it through the center vertically. This will be the length to cut the side borders. Place pins at the centers of all four sides of the quilt top, as well as in the center of each side border strip. Pin the side borders to the quilt top first, matching the center pins. Using a ¼″ seam allowance, sew the borders to the quilt top and press toward the borders.

Measure horizontally across the center of the quilt top including the side borders. This will be the length to cut the top and bottom borders. Repeat, pinning, sewing, and pressing.

BACKING

Plan on making the backing a minimum of 8″ longer and wider than the quilt top. Piece, if necessary. Trim the selvages before you piece to the desired size.

To economize, piece the back from any leftover quilting fabrics or blocks in your collection.

BATTING

The type of batting to use is a personal decision; consult your local quilt shop. Cut batting 8″ longer and wider than the quilt top. Note that the batting choice will affect how much quilting is necessary for the quilt. Check the manufacturer's instructions to see how far apart the quilting lines can be.

LAYERING

Spread the backing wrong side up and tape the edges down with masking tape. (If you are working on carpet you can use T-pins to secure the backing to the carpet.) Center the batting on top, smoothing out any folds. Place the quilt top right side up on top of the batting and backing, making sure it is centered.

BASTING

Basting keeps the quilt "sandwich" layers from shifting while you are quilting.

If you plan to machine quilt, pin-baste the quilt layers together with safety pins placed about 3″–4″ apart. Begin basting in the center and move toward the edges in first vertical then horizontal rows. Try not to pin directly on the intended quilting lines.

If you plan to hand quilt, baste the layers together with thread using a long needle and light-colored thread. Knot one end of the thread. Using stitches approximately the length of the needle, begin in the center and move out toward the edges in vertical and horizontal rows approximately 4″ apart. Add two diagonal rows of basting.

QUILTING

Quilting, whether by hand or machine, enhances the pieced or appliquéd design of the quilt. You may choose to quilt in-the-ditch, echo the pieced or appliquéd motifs, use patterns from quilting design books and stencils, or do your own free-motion quilting. Remember to check the batting manufacturer's recommendations for how close together the quilting lines must be. For more thoughts on quilting, see Quilting Makes the Quilt (page 28).

BINDING

Trim excess batting and backing so the edges are even with the quilt top edges.

Double-Fold Straight-Grain Binding

Cut the binding strips as specified in the project directions and piece them together with diagonal seams to make a continuous binding strip. Trim the seam allowance to ¼″. Press the seams open.

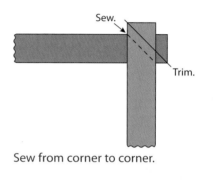

Sew from corner to corner.

Completed diagonal seam

Press the entire strip in half lengthwise with wrong sides together. With raw edges even, pin the binding to the front edge of the quilt starting a few inches away from a corner, but leave the first few inches of the binding unstitched. Start sewing, using a ¼″ seam allowance.

Stop ¼″ away from the first corner (see Step 1), and back-stitch one stitch. Lift the presser foot and needle. Rotate the quilt one-quarter turn. Fold the binding at a right angle so it extends straight above the quilt and the fold forms a 45° angle in the corner (see Step 2). Then bring the binding strip down even with the edge of the quilt (see Step 3). Begin sewing at the folded edge. Repeat in the same manner at all corners. Continue stitching until you are back near the beginning of the binding strip.

Finishing the Binding Ends

After stitching around the quilt, fold under the beginning tail of the binding strip ¼″ so that the raw edge will be inside the binding after it is turned to the back of the quilt. Place the end tail of the binding strip inside the beginning folded end. Continue to attach the binding and stitch slightly beyond the starting stitches. Trim away the excess binding. Fold the binding over the raw quilt edges to the quilt back and hand stitch in place, mitering the corners.

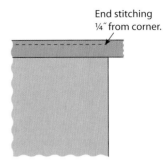

End stitching ¼″ from corner.

Step 1

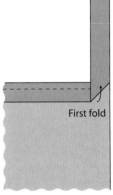

First fold

Step 2

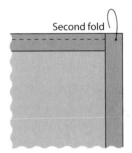

Second fold

Step 3

QUILT COLOR LIST

The following are the specific colors that were used—or could be used—for the project quilts as pictured in this book. The colors listed here are Robert Kaufman Kona Cotton Solids. Please note that colors come and go at the manufacturer's discretion, and a color listed here may no longer be available.

Feel free to pick and choose from these colors, or skip them altogether and replace them with your favorite hand-dyes, batiks, or near-solids.

CITY RAIN (page 35)

- Charcoal
- Leftover scraps from all the other projects

CITY TRAIL (page 41)

- Amber
- Apricot
- Brick
- Brown
- Burgundy
- Butterscotch
- Cayenne
- Celadon
- Celery
- Cheddar
- Cocoa
- Crimson
- Everglade
- Garnet
- Gold
- Khaki
- Mocha
- Nutmeg
- Ochre
- Paprika
- Sable
- Spice
- Yarrow

CITY BRIDGE (page 47)

- Colors are listed in the project instructions.

CITY WOODS (page 53)

- Basil
- Brown
- Caramel
- Crème
- Grass Green
- Ivy
- Laurel
- Sand
- Spruce
- Straw
- Wheat
- Zucchini

CITY HALL (page 59)

- Bright Pink
- Burgundy
- Cardinal
- Cerise
- Chinese Red
- Cinnamon
- Coral
- Melon
- Pomegranate
- Red
- Rich Red
- Ruby
- Tangerine
- Tomato
- Wine

CITY TRAFFIC (page 63)

- Berry
- Dark Violet
- Eggplant
- Hibiscus
- Ocean
- Pacific
- Pepper
- Purple
- Raisin
- Royal
- Sour Apple
- Spearmint

CITY SKY (page 67)

- Aqua
- Azure
- Banana
- Blue
- Bubble Gum
- Butterscotch
- Champagne
- Charcoal
- Coffee
- Curry
- Daffodil
- Dusty Blue
- Magenta
- Maize
- Melon
- Mustard
- Navy
- Ocean
- Petunia
- Regatta
- Violet
- Berry
- Dark Violet
- Eggplant
- Hibiscus
- Ocean
- Pacific
- Pepper
- Purple
- Raisin
- Royal
- Sour Apple
- Spearmint

CITY LOFT (page 71)

- Chinese Red
- Essex Linen—White

CITY RECYCLING (page 75)

- Aqua
- Avocado
- Bayou
- Bone
- Cactus
- Cardinal
- Clover
- Cornflower
- Everglade
- Evergreen
- Glacier
- Green Tea
- Holly
- Ice Frappe
- Jade Green
- Jungle
- Kelly
- Lake
- Lapis
- Laurel
- Mint
- Mocha
- Ocean
- Palm
- Parsley
- Peridot
- Pistachio
- Raisin
- Robin Egg
- Ruby
- Sable
- Sage
- Sand
- Snow
- Spearmint
- Surf
- Tarragon
- Taupe
- Teal Blue
- Tomato
- Wheat

CITY BEAT (page 81)

- Amber
- Berry
- Brick
- Burgundy
- Butterscotch
- Canary
- Cerise
- Charcoal
- Chocolate
- Cinnamon
- Coal
- Coffee
- Dark Violet
- Eggplant
- Evergreen
- Fern
- Garnet
- Hibiscus
- Magenta
- Mocha
- Mulberry
- Navy
- Nightfall
- Orange
- Papaya
- Pepper
- Plum
- School Bus
- Tangerine

CITY ELECTRIC (page 87)

- Ash
- Cadet
- Celery
- Charcoal
- Coal
- Green Tea
- Herb
- Ivory
- Olive
- Pale Mint
- Raffia
- Raisin
- Slate
- Snow
- Stone
- Tan
- White
- Windsor

CITY LAKE (page 93)

- Amethyst
- Asparagus
- Bright Periwinkle
- Caribbean
- Cloud
- Clover
- Cornflower
- Crocus
- Emerald
- Evergreen
- Fern
- Forest
- Honey Dew
- Lavender
- Maize
- Ocean
- Orchid
- Periwinkle
- Petunia
- Pistachio
- Thistle

ABOUT THE AUTHOR

Cherri House loves quilts. At a young age she was exposed to clothing construction by her master seamstress of a mom, who could sew anything … anything! Her mom's skill, and Cherri's first encounter with quiltmaking, inspired her to become the quilter that she is today. Sewing is in her genes, she says. She has practiced her craft over the years while wearing many different hats—those of single mother, full-time jobholder, and full-time quilter.

After her youngest daughter moved away, she said, "Hey, world, it's Cherry House Quilts time," and the world responded positively. Cherri gathers inspiration from life and looks for beauty in all her surroundings. She loves taking things she sees in her everyday routine and making them into art. It's with that attitude that she has undertaken this, her second book.

Cherri is grateful for the ability to quilt and the opportunities that have blessed her life. She says she wouldn't be where she is today without her mom, LDK; her four beautiful children, Luke, Elizabeth, Ashlee, and Melissa; and her four lovely grandbabies.

She thanks you for your continued support!

Photo by Lizzy House

Cherri's website: cherryhousequilts.com

Also available by Cherri House:

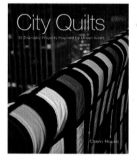

RESOURCES

Bernina USA
Sewing machines
berninausa.com

C&T Publishing
Ultimate 3-in-1 Color Tool
ctpub.com

Cherrywood Fabrics
cherrywoodfabrics.com

Creative Grids
Quilting rulers
creativegridsusa.com

David Jones
davidlouisjones.com

The Electric Quilt Company
EQ7 quilt design software
electricquilt.com

• **EZ Quilting by Wrights**
Tri-Recs Tools acrylic triangle ruler set
simplicity.com

Hoffman California–International Fabrics
hoffmanfabrics.com

Moda Fabrics
unitednotions.com

Olfa
Rotary cutting mats, rotary cutters
olfa.com

Omnigrid
Rotary cutting rulers, rotary cutting mats
dritz.com/brands/omnigrid

Robert Kaufman Fabrics
Kona Cotton Solids
robertkaufman.com

Sulky of America
Thread
sulky.com

The Warm Company
Warm & Natural cotton batting
warmcompany.com

Teaching: A Two-Way Street

Teaching on a national level has been a wonderful new experience for me. I loved meeting you, seeing your quilts, and visiting your cities. One of the most interesting aspects of speaking and teaching has been the question-and-answer portion of events. Your genuine inquiries gave me an opportunity to reflect on the work I do and what I was presenting. I took your questions to heart, and I wanted to share some of the more frequently asked questions.

Q: Do you have any formal art training?

A: No, I was trained and worked as a florist for years, which has greatly influenced how I design. Though I've had no formal art training, I have always had a love of color and design.

Q: Do you have any formal quilt training?

A: No, my mother taught me to sew, and I taught myself to quilt through television programs (thank you, Alex Anderson) and books (thank you, Mary Ellen Hopkins).

Q: How many colors should be in a particular quilt?

A: I generally have no idea; I add whatever I think a quilt needs in terms of color. I realize, though, that this isn't the answer you are seeking—the majority of you would rather know exactly what to buy than to read an instruction such as "Buy three yards of assorted blue solids." As a compromise, this book includes a Quilt Color List (page 108) that tells exactly which fabric colors I used for the quilts shown in this book.

Q: Why do you love solids so much?

A: They are timeless, they work much like paint, they take on the appearance of colored glass, and they are beautiful.

Q: Will you continue to create more city quilts?

A: Yes!

Q: Tell us about your quilt studio.

A: I don't have a formal sewing studio; I sew in a corner of my bedroom. A dedicated work space would be great, but until I have the studio of my dreams, my little corner is great!

Q: How do you feel about following a particular methodology?

A: I believe in mastering the basics, having a solid foundation in the fundamentals of sewing and quilting. I'm not a fan of being compelled to follow the latest trend of "musts" or "must nots."

stashBOOKS®

fabric arts for a handmade lifestyle

If you're craving beautiful authenticity in a time of mass-production...Stash Books is for you. Stash Books is a line of how-to books celebrating fabric arts for a handmade lifestyle. Backed by C&T Publishing's solid reputation for quality, Stash Books will inspire you with contemporary designs, clear and simple instructions, and engaging photography.

www.stashbooks.com